CROCHET

CROCHET

PENNY HILL

SERIES EDITOR: ROSEMARY WILKINSON

CHARTWELL BOOKS, INC.

ENGLISH CROCHET TERMS ARE USED THROUGHOUT

American terms which are different are as follows:

U.K.	U.S.
Double crochet - **dc**	Single crochet - **sc**
Half treble - **htr**	Half double crochet - **hdc**
Treble - **tr**	Double crochet - **dc**
Double treble - **dtr**	Treble - **tr**
Triple treble - **trtr**	Double treble - **dtr**
Quadruple treble - **qtr**	Triple treble - **trtr**
Miss	Skip
Tension	Gauge
Work straight	Work even
Yarn round hook - **yrh**	Yarn over - **yo**

Note: Imperial and metric measurements are not direct equivalents, so always follow only one set in a particular method.

Published by
CHARTWELL BOOKS, INC.
A Division of BOOK SALES, INC.
110 Enterprise Avenue
Secaucus, New Jersey 07094

Created and produced by
Rosemary Wilkinson and Malcolm Saunders Publishing Ltd
4 Lonsdale Square, London N1 1EN

ISBN 0-7858-0007-7

Printed and bound in
Hong Kong

Illustrations: Terry Evans
Design: Ming Cheung
Cover photograph: by courtesy of DMC, 10, Avenue Ledru-Rollin,
F-75579 Paris, Cedex 12, France

Contents

Introduction

Crochet gained popularity during the nineteenth century as a quick method of copying the intricate needle and pillow lace designs that were the height of fashion. The results proved so satisfactory that a whole cottage industry sprang up to fulfil the demand. However, the vogue passed and crochet almost disappeared until it was revived through the renewed interest in handicrafts in the twentieth century. Today enthusiasts abound, especially among the young, as crochet has become a designer favourite for the latest fashions. Crochet also mixes well with other fabrics, for example, as a lacy edging to a window blind or around a tablecloth.

As a craft, crochet is ideal: you can start with only minimal expenditure, all you need is a ball of yarn or cotton thread and a crochet hook. If you've never tried crochet before, now is the time to start with the help of this technique-lead book. Everything you need to know to begin the craft is here, described and illustrated in easy-to-follow steps. There's also a variety of different types of crochet, such as filet crochet or Tunisian crochet for those who are already familiar with the craft and are looking to increase their expertise.

Part 1:
EQUIPMENT

Yarns

Yarn is divided into two main types - natural and synthetic. Natural yarn is more expensive, but is more pleasant to wear and easier to handle when knitting. Synthetic yarn is cheaper but stronger and lasts longer.

Natural yarns

Wool which is easily available, long lasting and very warm comes from sheep which are bred for their fleeces. Merino sheep have the most abundant and highest quality yarn.

Mohair yarn comes from goats which originated in Turkey. The long brushed fibres are extremely thick and warm.

Angora is an expensive soft and warm yarn which comes from the short haired albino rabbit of the same name.

Cashmere, the most expensive and luxurious of yarns, is spun with a high percentage of wool and comes from a special breed of goat.

Alpaca is a soft high quality fibre with a slight hairiness which comes from a species of camel related to the llama.

Silk knitting yarns are heavy and therefore expensive, but mixed with other fibres produce a strong durable thread.

Cotton is a strong, non allergenic, easy to wash and wear yarn that has little elasticity. Cotton thread for crochet ranges from very fine to thick string or even cotton fabric torn into strips. The finer the yarn, the finer the hook and the more delicate the work. Fine cotton, which comes on small spools, is mainly used for lace collars and filet crochet. Thicker cotton can be used for garments. It is available as thin as 3 or 4 ply or as thick as Aran weight. Cotton fabric can be used by cutting it up into bias strips and either sewing them together, or for added interest, knotting the ends securely. This can then be used for making washable crocheted rugs.

Linen comes from the flax plant, is stronger than cotton and is usually blended with wool for more elasticity.

Synthetic yarns

Man-made yarns have improved dramatically over the last few years, these yarns are no longer lifeless with little elasticity. With clever combinations of synthetic and natural fibres, fashionable, strong and lightweight yarns can be produced, their cost compares favourably with more expensive natural fibres.

The thickness of yarn

Yarn is formed by twisting together a number of strands, or plys, of fibre. The terms 3-ply, 4-ply, double knitting, Aran and Chunky are only general descriptions for yarns as plys can vary in thickness, so great care has to be taken when substituting yarns. Always check that the substitute yarn produces the correct tension (see page 42).

The texture of yarn

During the spinning process the fibres can be fused together at different rates. Bouclé is produced by introducing one ply at a faster rate than the other two, so that it buckles up. Mohair is a brushed loop yarn, giving it a fluffy appearance. Slub yarns have at least one ply that varies in thickness producing an uneven look. Tweed effects are formed by adding coloured blips to longer fibres.

Reading a ball-band

The printed band around a ball of crochet cotton gives various pieces of useful information on laundering the yarn and which crochet hook is suitable.

The information is given graphically through symbols but also with brief explanatory text. Below are the most common international symbols used:

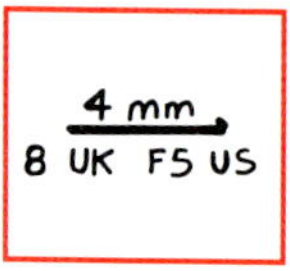

The suggested appropriate hook size. A crochet pattern will also stipulate a hook size for working the pattern. If this is different from the manufacturer's recommendation, follow the size given in the pattern, as this will have been used to produce the specific tension for the pattern.

Hand wash only.

Machine washable at stated temperature and stated wash program. Temperatures for cottons are shown without a bar underneath the symbol; for synthetics with a single bar and for wools with a broken bar.

May be bleached (with chlorine).

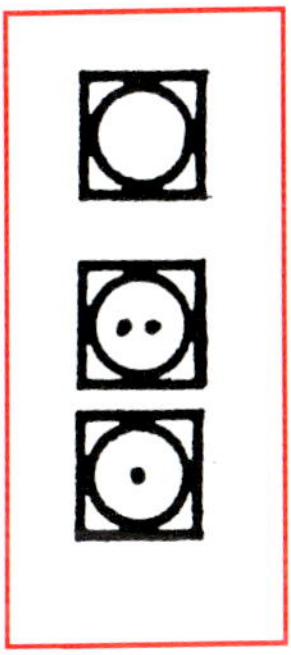

May be tumble dried. Where dots appear in the symbol, two dots means a high heat setting; one dot a low heat setting.

Iron with cool iron.

Iron with warm iron.

Iron with hot iron.

May be dry cleaned - the letter within the circle indicates which solutions may be used. Show the label to your dry cleaner.

A cross through any symbol means DO NOT.

Hooks and related items

All that is needed to produce a piece of crochet is a hook, although you may find some other items rather useful.

Crochet hooks

Hooks are available in plastic, steel or aluminium.

A **steel hook** is used with very fine cotton, linen or silk yarns and sometimes 3-ply yarn. The length is 5in(13cm) and the sizes available are 14-5 US (0.60mm-1.75mm metric).

Aluminium hooks are used for working wool, thicker cotton and synthetic yarns, lightweight to heavy. The hooks are 6in(15cm) long and available in sizes B-K US (2.00mm-7.00mm metric).

A **plastic hook** is used with rug wool or fabric strips to make rugs. It is hollow, 5in(13cm) long and comes in size P US(8.00mm-10.00mm metric).

The chart opposite shows the equivalent American, British and metric hook sizes.

US	METRIC	UK
14 steel	0.60mm	
12 steel	0.75mm	
10 steel	1.00mm	
6 steel	1.50mm	
5 steel	1.75mm	
B/1	2.00mm	14
C/2	2.50mm	12
D/3	3.00mm	10
E/4	3.50mm	9
F/5	4.00mm	8
G/6	4.50mm	7
H/8	5.00mm	6
I/9	5.50mm	5
J/10	6.00mm	4
	6.50mm	3
K/10 ½	7.00mm	2

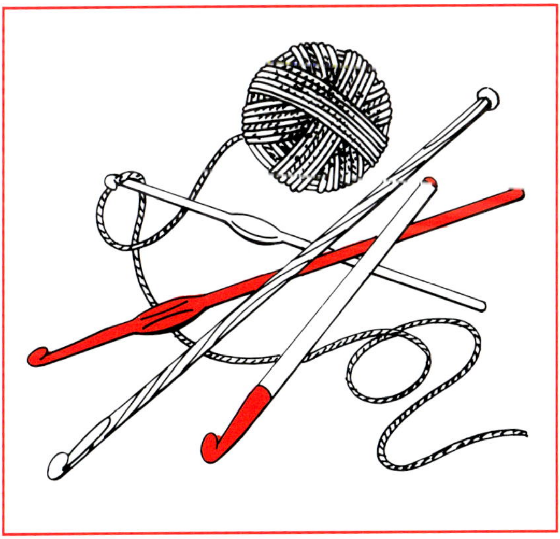

Tricot hooks

A tricot needle or hook is used for Tunisian crochet. This is similar to an ordinary crochet hook but it is longer to accommodate a whole row of stitches and has a bobble at the opposite end to the hook to prevent the stitches from falling off. These hooks range in size from B-P US(2.00mm to 10.00mm metric) and are 12in (30cm) long.

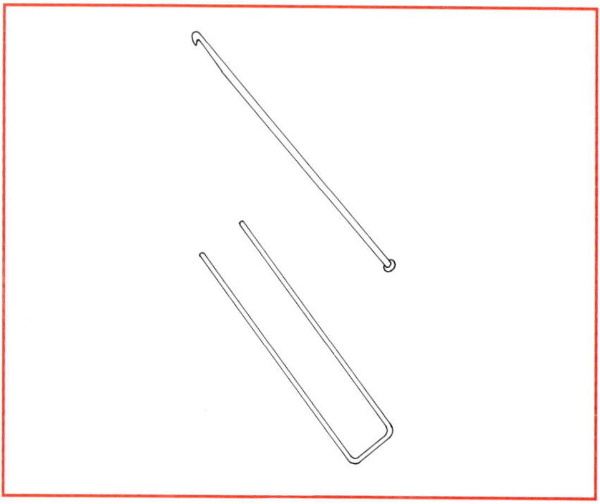

Two prong forks

Two prong forks are used for Hairpin crochet to form a light airy fabric. The size of the fork varies according to the width.

Ancillary equipment

Tape measure

Choose a strong measure that cannot stretch as this can distort your measurements. Always use either inches or centimetres.

Scissors

These can be small but must be sharp as some yarns are very strong and cannot be broken.

Pins

Pins can disappear in the crochet if they are too small, so choose long ones with coloured glass heads.

Sewing needles

Use needles with large eyes and blunt ends for sewing up - sharp needles can split the yarn and weaken it.

Part 2:
TECHNIQUES

Before you Begin

How to hold the crochet hook and yarn

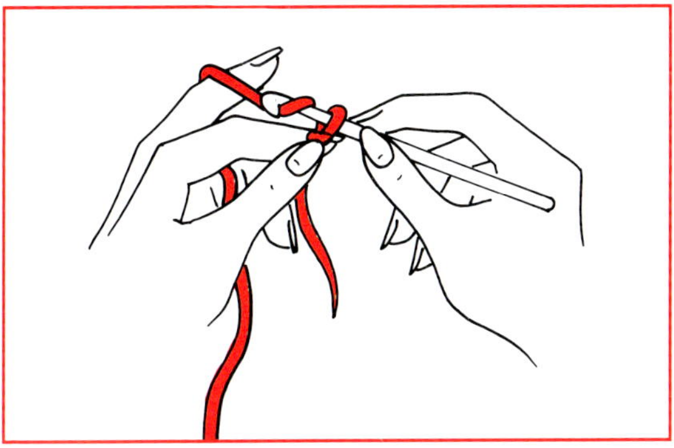

Hold the crochet hook in the right hand, between the thumb and index finger, placing the thumb on the flat part of the hook. The yarn passes over the index and middle finger of the left hand, under the ring finger and around the little finger, folded towards the palm of the hand.

Note to left-handers

Left-handed people may find it easier to trace the diagrams from the book, turn the tracing paper over and follow them from the wrong side. Alternatively, place the book in front of a mirror and work from the reflection.

Making the first chain stitch (ch)

1 Hold the end of the yarn between the thumb and index finger of the left hand, with the working yarn

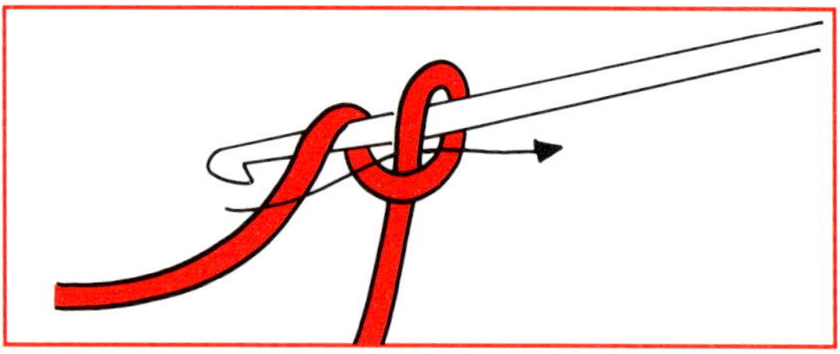

fixed between the ring and little fingers of the left hand. Insert the hook under the thread from right to left and twist the hook through 360° to make a loop. Insert the crochet hook from front to back under the yarn.

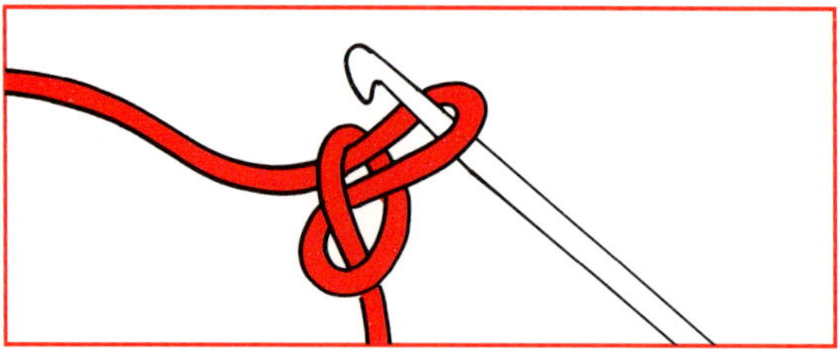

2 Pull the hook through the loop to make the first chain stitch (ch).

Making a length of chain

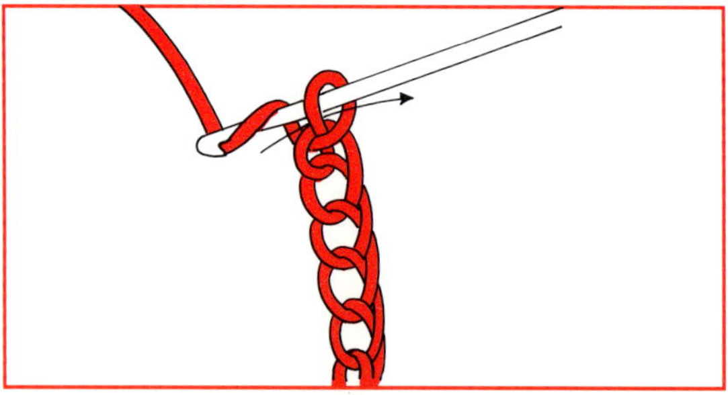

This is the starting point for all work. Make the first ch, holding the crochet hook horizontally. Then using the hook and looping it anticlockwise under the yarn, catch the yarn held in the left hand in the slot of the hook - this step is called yarn round hook (yrh). Draw the hook and the yarn in it through the loop (lp) already on the hook, which draws out a new ch. Continue in this way to produce a length of chain. This is called the base chain.

Basic Stitches

The following stitches are described being made into the base chain, i.e. as the first row of crochet stitches. The method for subsequent rows is described on page 24.

Slip stitch (ss)

This stitch has very little depth and therefore is usually used to move from one position in a row to another without adding a visible stitch. It is also used for joining rows when working in rounds.

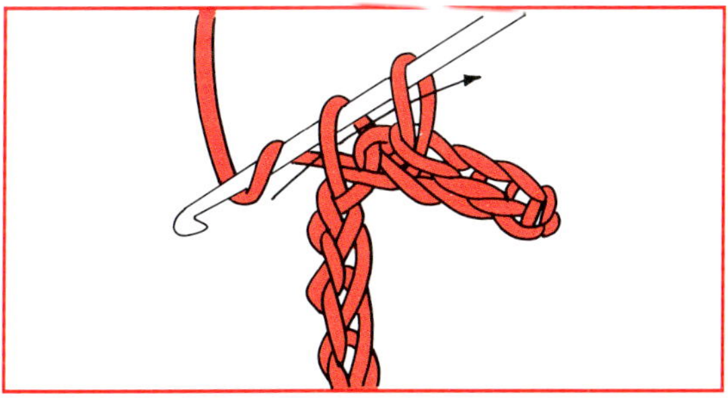

Miss first ch. * Insert the hook into the top of the next ch, yrh, draw the loop just formed through the chain and loop on hook in one movement. Repeat from * to end.

Double crochet (dc)

This is the shortest of the crochet stitches. When worked in solid rows, it produces a firm, densely stitched fabric.

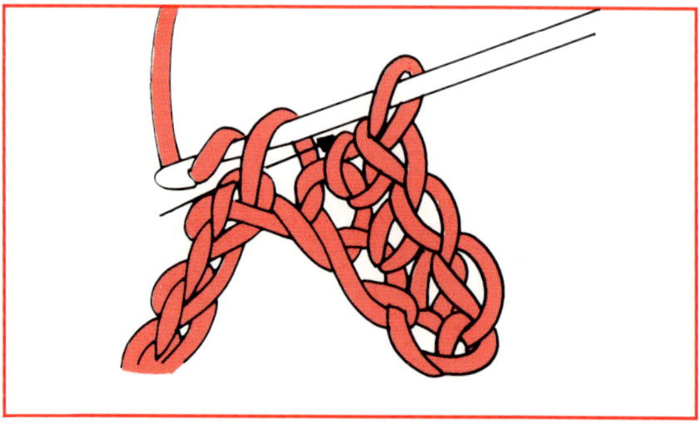

1 Miss first 2 ch. Insert the hook into the top of the next ch, yrh and draw through a loop, so there are 2 lps on hook.

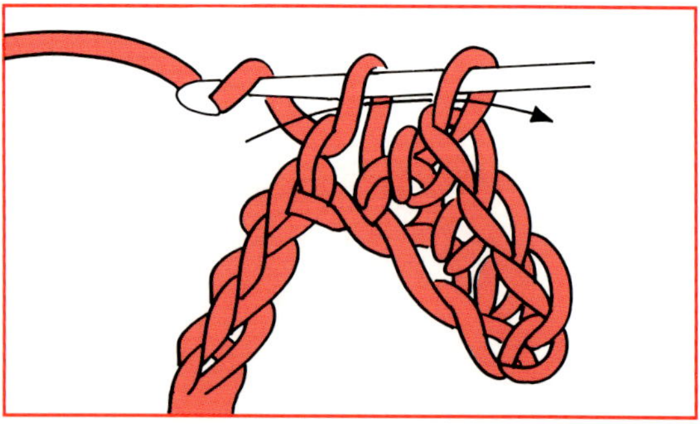

2 Yrh, draw the loop formed through both lps on the hook. Repeat these 2 steps to form each dc.

Square double crochet (dc)

Double crochet is not a square stitch, it is not as high as it is wide. If you are following a graph paper design and this will cause a problem, you can square the stitch. To do this, work as follows:

1 Insert the hook through the stitch below as usual, yrh, and draw through a loop (2 lps on hook).

2 Yrh, draw through the first loop (2 lps on hook), then yrh again and draw through both loops. This effectively puts a chain stitch in the middle of the row, adding the required extra height.

Half treble (htr)

These and the following stitches gradually increase in depth.

1 Miss first 2 ch. Yrh, insert the hook into the top of the next ch, yrh, and draw through a lp (3 lps on hook).

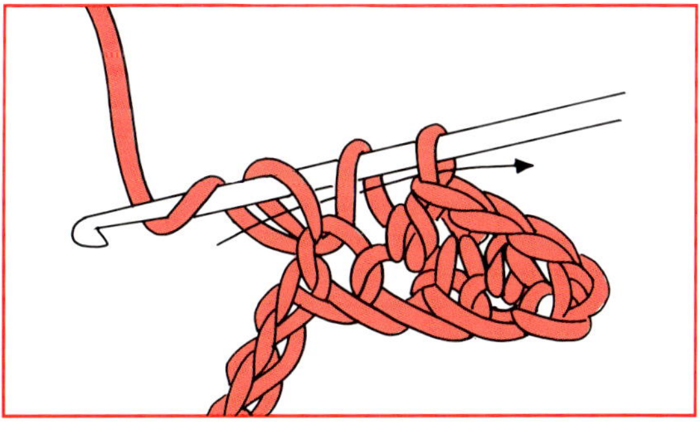

2 Yrh, and draw the loop formed through all 3 lps on hook. Repeat these 2 steps to form each htr.

Treble (tr)

This is the basic stitch used in "filet crochet" (see page 63).

1 Miss first 3 ch. Yrh, insert the hook into the top of the next ch, yrh and draw through a lp (3 lps on hook).

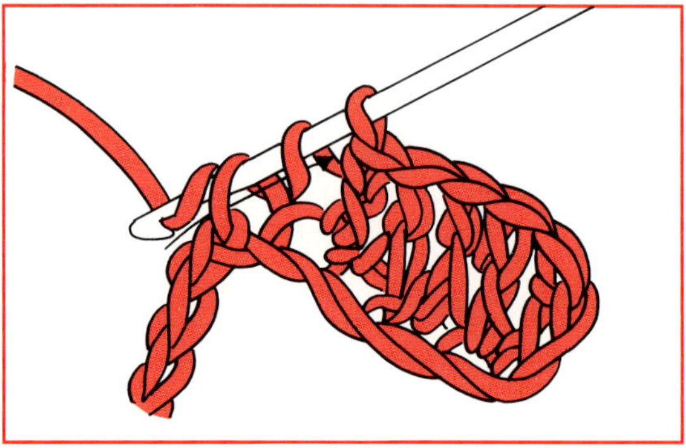

2 Yrh and draw the loop just formed through the first 2 lps on the hook.

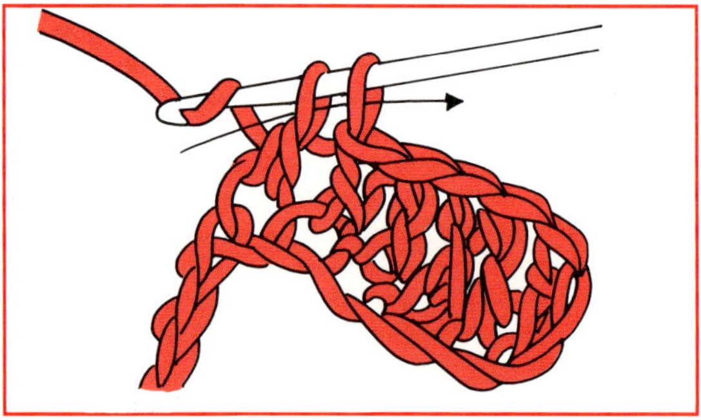

3 Yrh again and draw the loop formed through the last 2 lps on the hook, finishing the stitch. Repeat these 3 steps to form each tr.

Double treble (dtr)

This is a tall stitch which is used less frequently than the previous stitches.

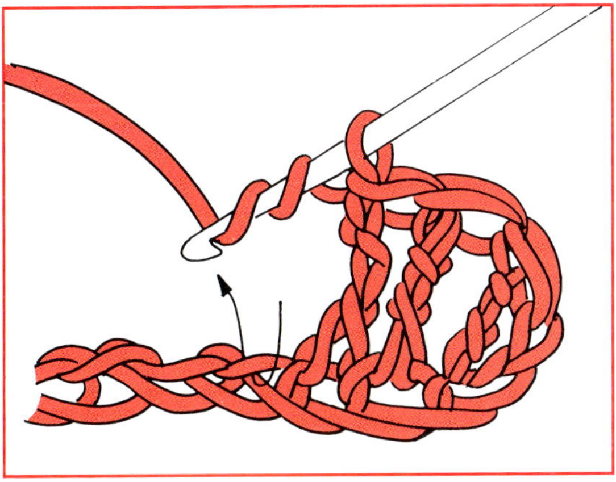

1 Miss first 4 ch. Wind yarn twice round hook, then insert the hook into the top of the next ch.

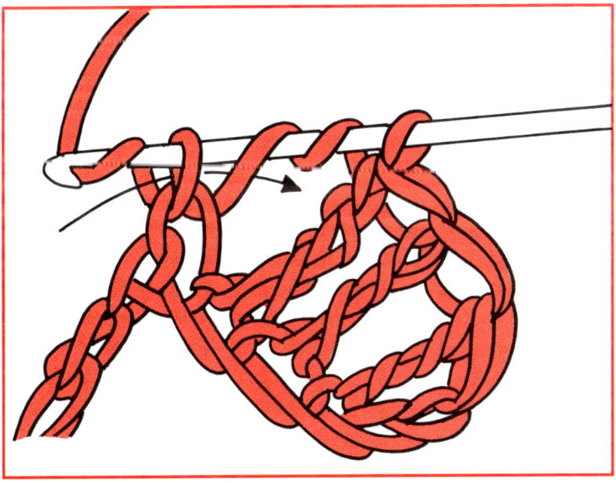

2 [Yrh and draw through the first 2 lps on hook] 3 times to complete the stitch.

Triple, quadruple or quintuple treble (trtr,quadtr or quintr)

A series of taller, less commonly used stitches.

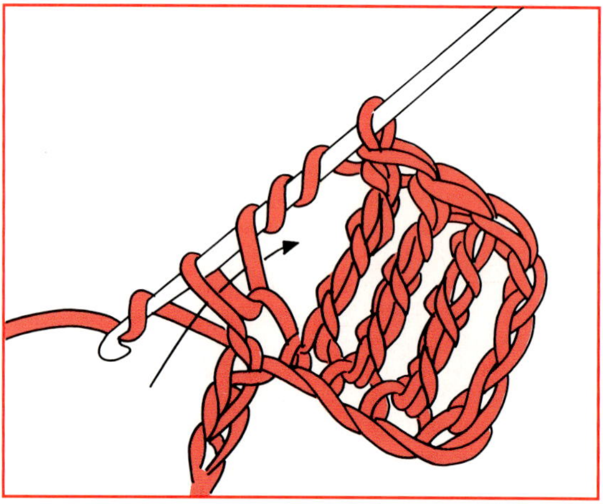

Miss the first 5 ch for triple treble, the first 6 ch for quadruple treble, or the first 7 ch for quintuple treble. Then, for each stitch, use the same method as for double treble: wind the yarn around the hook 3, 4 or 5 times (depending on the stitch), then insert the hook into the top of the stitch and work the instructions in the square brackets 4, 5 or 6 times.

Stitches into second and subsequent rows

The method for making all the above stitches into a row of previously formed stitches rather than into the base chain is identical except that the crochet hook is inserted into the top of the stitch in the previous row (which will look like a chain stitch). The method for starting a row is described on page 27.

Fancy Stitches

Popcorn stitch

A popcorn stitch is made from a group of identical stitches which are worked into the same stitch, then folded and drawn together at the top. It can be made from any basic stitch apart from a slip stitch.

To make a popcorn with 4 trebles

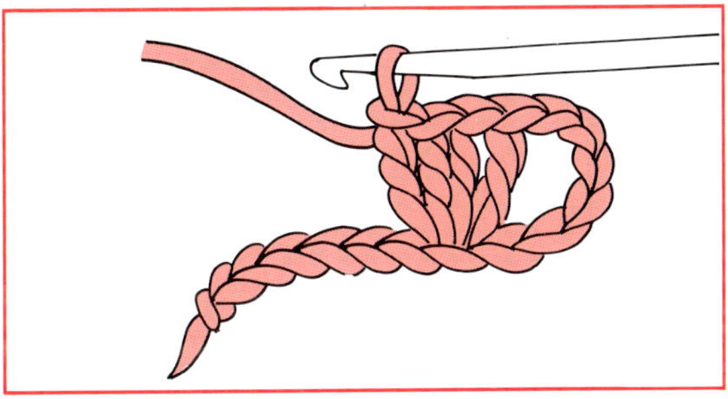

Work 4 tr into the same st.

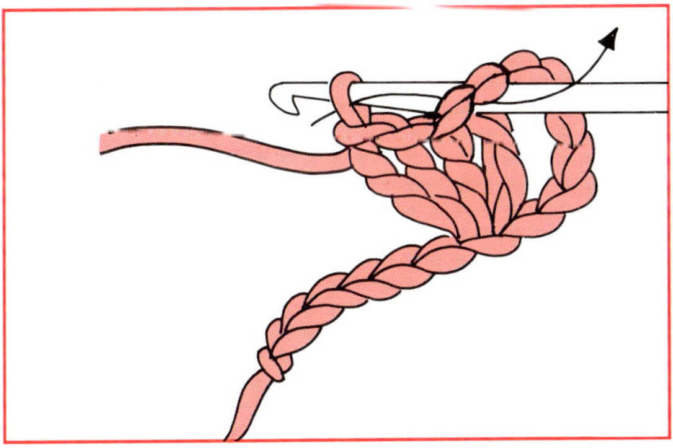

Take the hook out of the 4th tr, insert it through the top of the first tr, then back into the loop of the 4th tr.

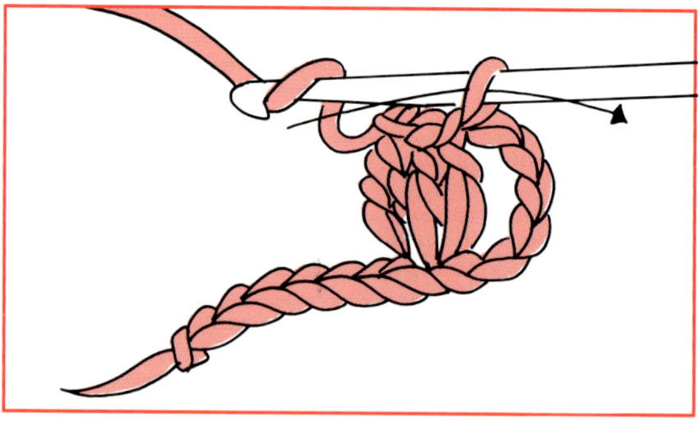

Pull the loop through the top of the first tr. The popcorn can now be "locked" with an extra ch st if required.

Bobbles

A bobble is made from a group of stitches worked into the same stitch, gathered together at the top.

To make a bobble with 3 trebles

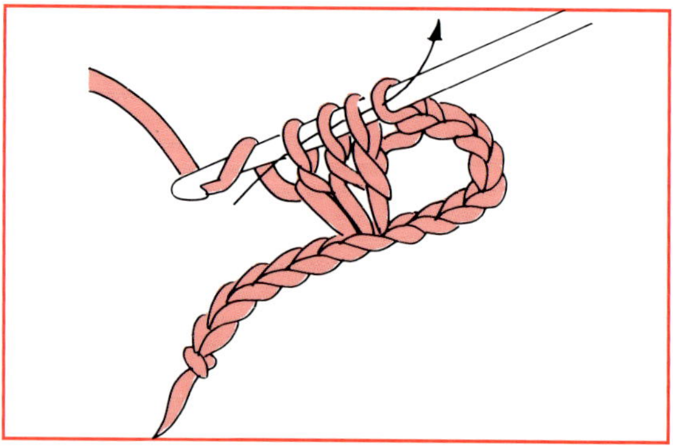

Leaving the last loop of each tr on hook, work 3 tr into the same stitch (4 lps on hook). Yrh and draw through all loops on hook.

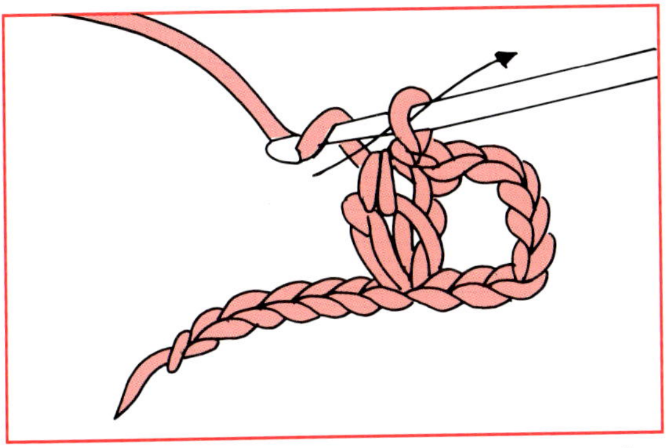

The bobble can now be "locked" with an extra ch st if required.

Working in Solid Rows

Rows are worked on top of one another, building up from the base chain. Each row starts with a number of chain in order to bring the work up to the height of the new row. These are called the turning chain. The number of turning chain depends on the type of stitch about to be worked, as listed in the following chart:

STITCH	TURNING CHAIN
slip stitch	0 chain
double crochet	2 chain
half treble	2 chain
treble	3 chain
double treble	4 chain
triple treble	5 chain
quadruple treble	6 chain
quintuple treble	7 chain

So, to work a solid row of trebles, work as follows:

Before the new row can begin, work 3 ch, this counts as the first tr and it brings the the hook to the height of the row of trebles.

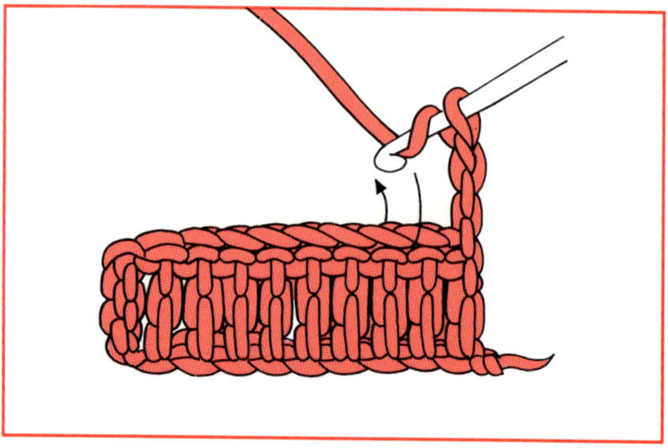

To make each st, insert the crochet hook under the two loops lying on top of each st of previous row.

Miss the first tr, then work 1 tr into each tr to end of row.

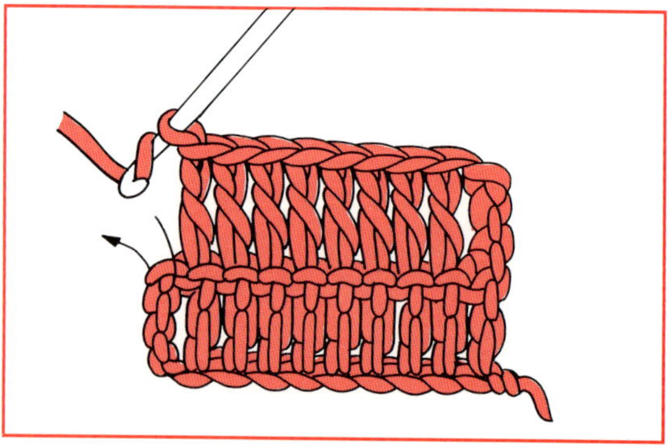

Subsequent rows are worked in exactly the same

way. The last stitch of each row is worked into the top of the turning ch of the previous row.

Working between the stitches

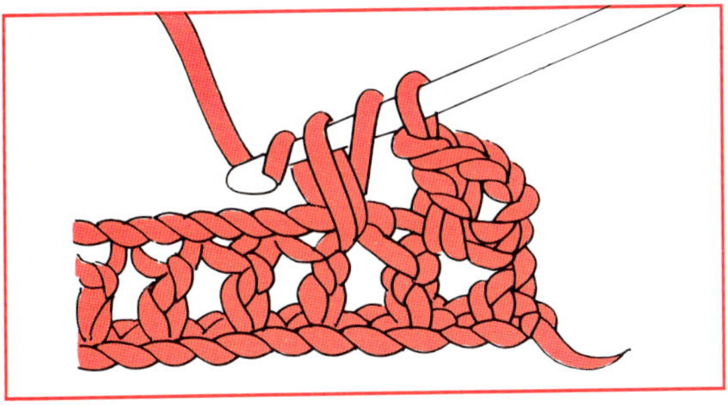

Sometimes a pattern will require you to make stitches between the stitches of the previous row, in which case, insert the hook underneath the whole stitch. This produces a more open fabric as the stitches are pushed apart.

Working under the front or back loop only

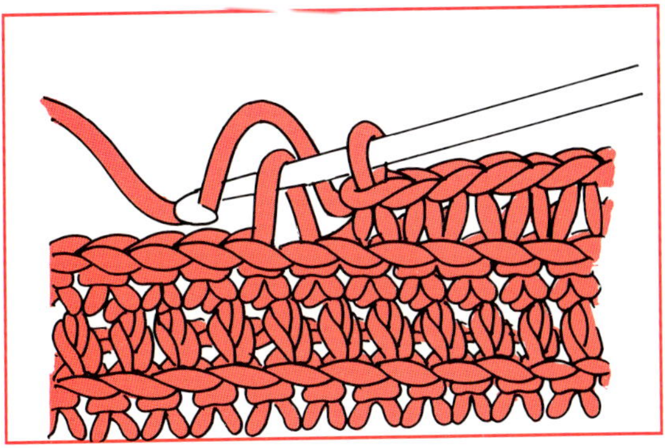

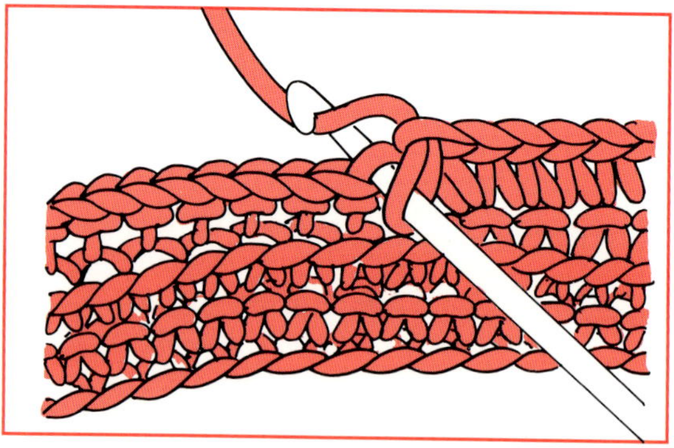

You may also need to work into the back loop only or the front loop only as shown in the diagrams. This will be stated in the instructions. Working consistently into the front or back loops only will produce rows of ridges, which can be used for working edges or trimmings into.

STARTING AND FINISHING

Joining in new yarn

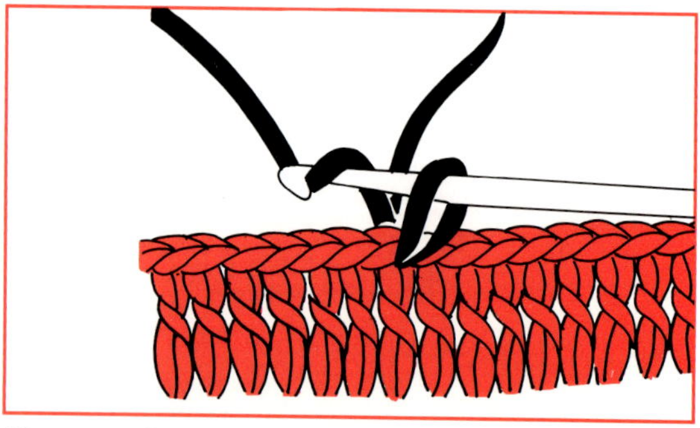

If you are fastening off, then starting a new ball of yarn in a different place, insert the hook into the appropriate place, draw a loop through and make a chain, then follow the instructions.

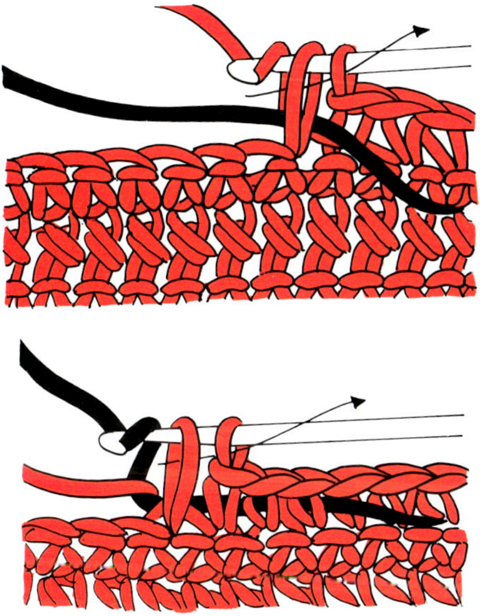

When joining a new ball of yarn in the middle of a row, lay the new yarn in advance across the tops of the stitches and work over it.

After the change-over work over the end of the previous yarn.

Finishing off

To fasten off the working yarn permanently, make one chain, cut the yarn about 2in (5cm) away from the hook, draw the end through the chain and tighten gently. Darn the loose end into the back of the work.

Changing colour

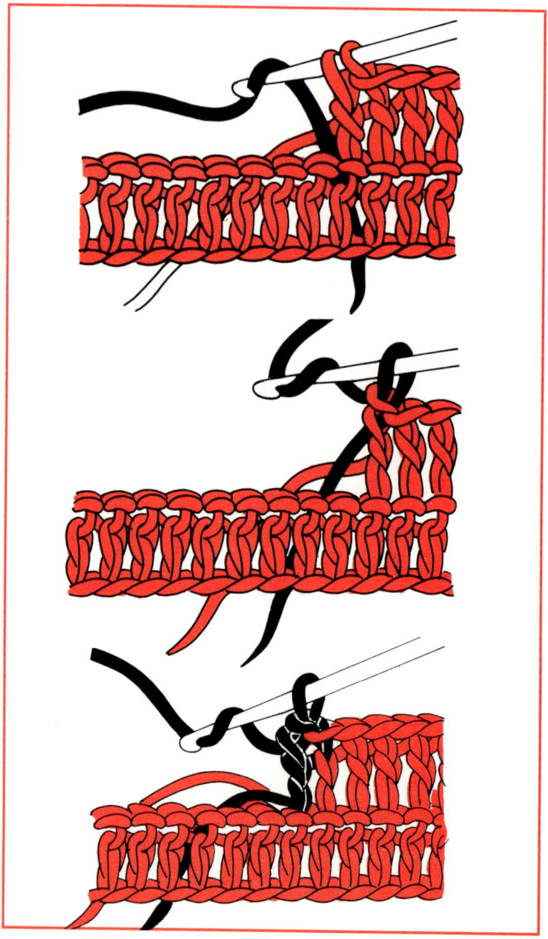

To join in a new colour in the middle of a row, pick up the new colour before you complete the last stitch in the old colour, so that the loop on the hook is in the new colour ready for the next stitch.

When working in alternate colours, carry the old colour along the top of the row below and crochet the new colour over it. It will then be in the correct position when you need to pick it up again.

INCREASING

Simple increase

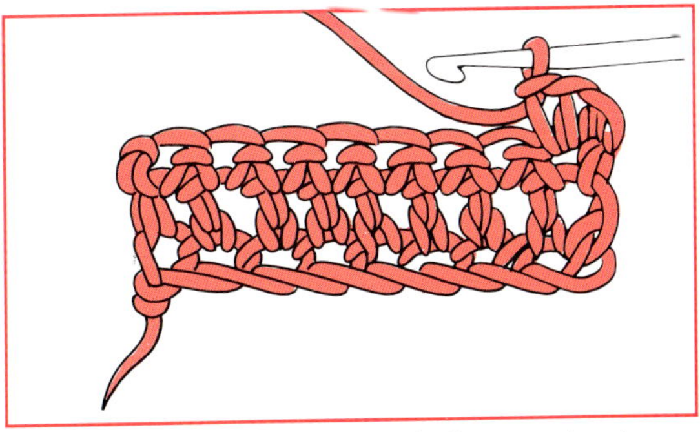

To increase 1 stitch at each end of a row, simply

work 2 sts into the stitch next to the end stitch at each end of the row.

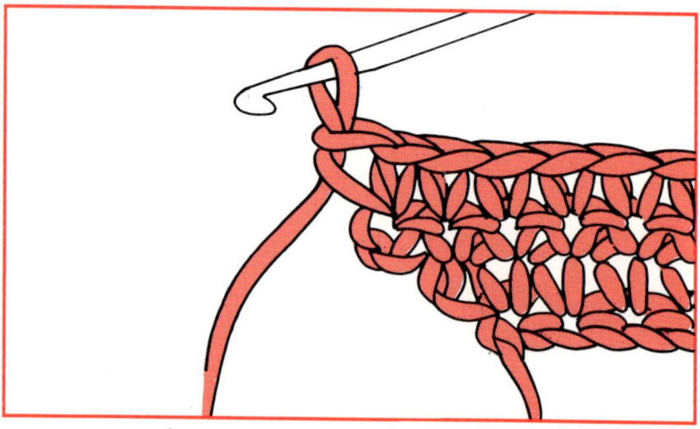

If the number of stitches to be increased is 1 stitch every row, work 2 sts into the first or the last stitch of every row.

Adding stitches at the beginning of a row

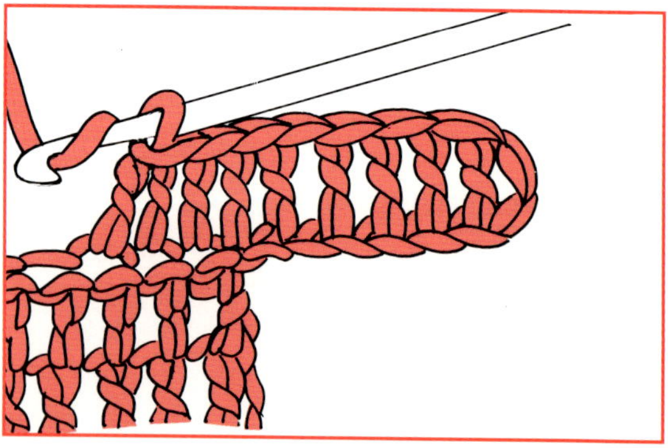

Make the same number of chain as stitches to be increased, plus the number of chain required for turning. Continue in pattern across the chain, then the stitches of the row.

Adding stitches at the end of the row

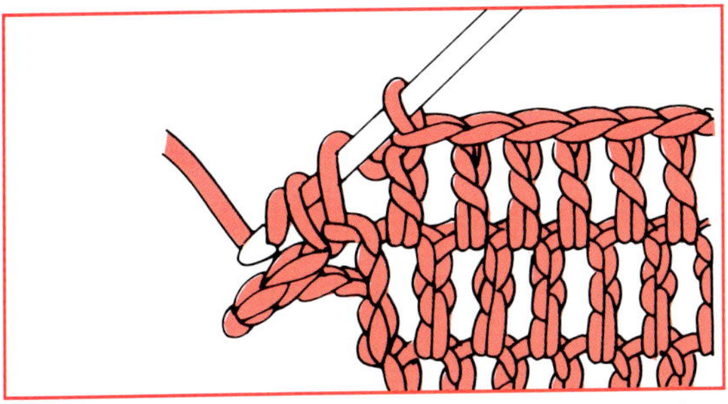

To keep increased stitches level, make provision for these sts at the beginning of previous row. Make same number of ch as sts required, ss over these ch and continue in pattern. On the next row continue to end of row.

Single increase in the middle of a row

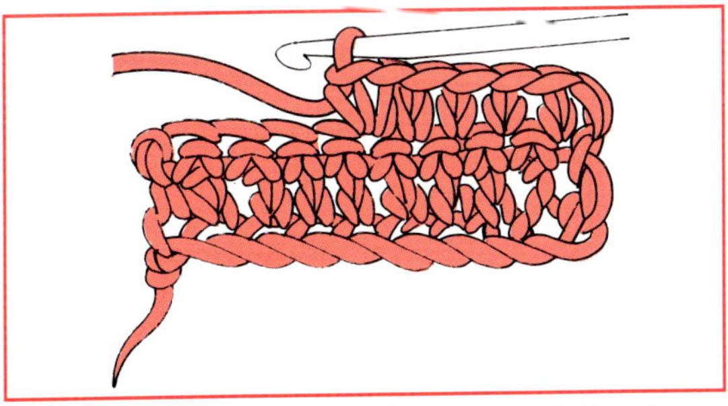

To increase in the middle of a row, work 2 sts into the same st.

Double increase in the middle of a row

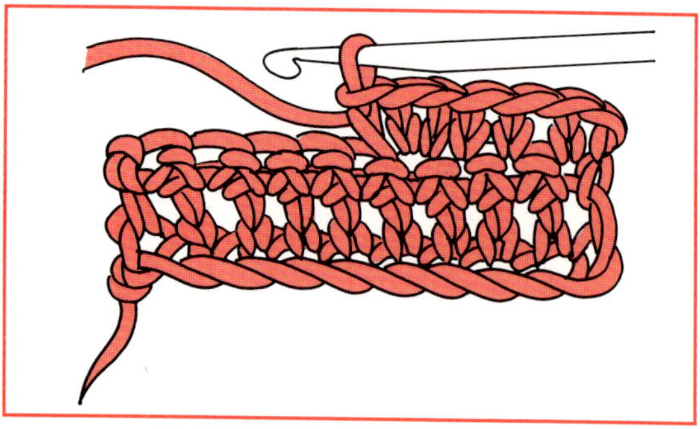

To increase 2 sts in the middle of a row, work 3 sts in the same st. If the increase is to be regular and symmetrical choose a central stitch and work 2 sts into one st either side of the central st.

DECREASING

Simple decrease

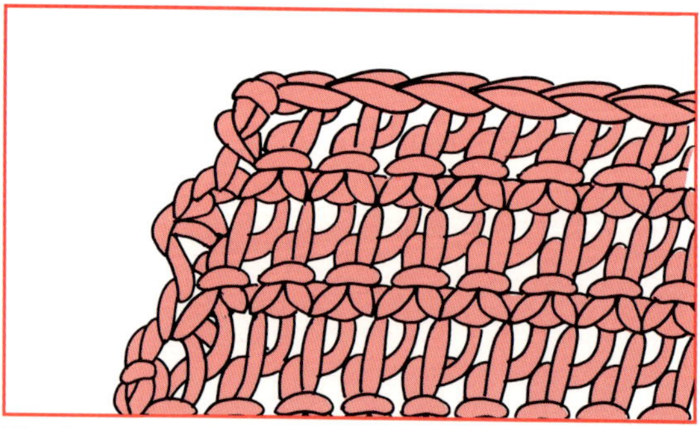

To decrease a st at the end (lefthand edge) of a row, work to the last 2 sts, miss next st, work into last st, then turn.

To decrease a st at the beginning (righthand edge) of a row, work the turning ch, miss the second stitch, then continue normally.

Decreasing a number of sts at the end of the row

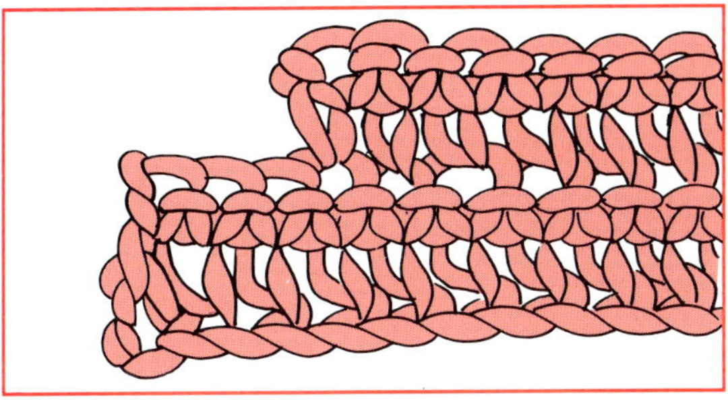

Leave the number of sts to be decreased unworked, turn and work the turning ch for the next row.

Decreasing a number of sts at the beginning of the row

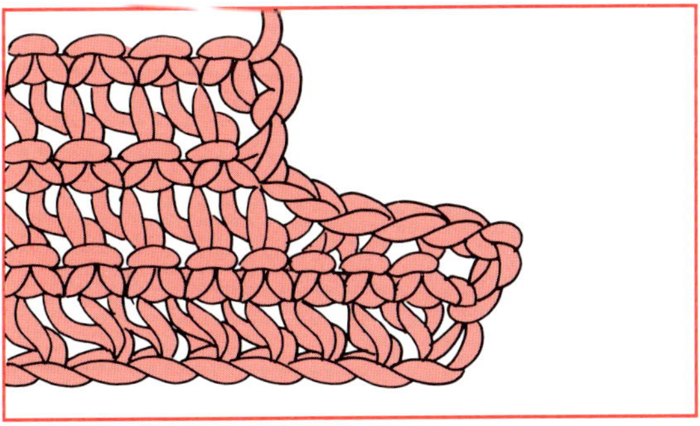

Slip stitch over the number of stitches to be

decreased plus an extra stitch, work the turning ch, then continue in pattern.

Simple decreasing in the middle of a row

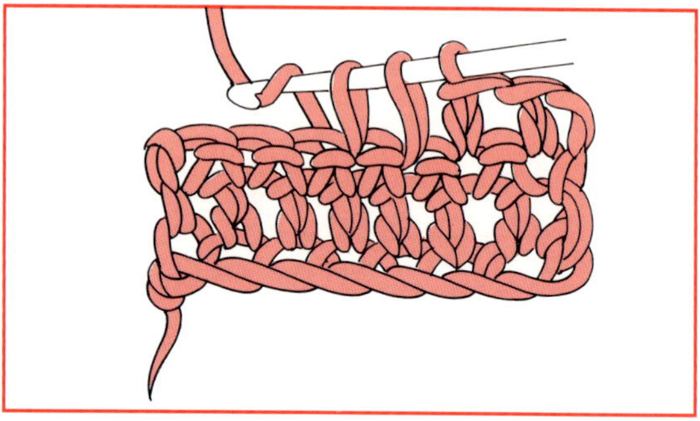

To decrease a stitch in the middle of a row, work 2 sts without completing them, leaving all 3 loops on hook, yrh and draw through all the loops together.

Decreasing two stitches in the middle of a row

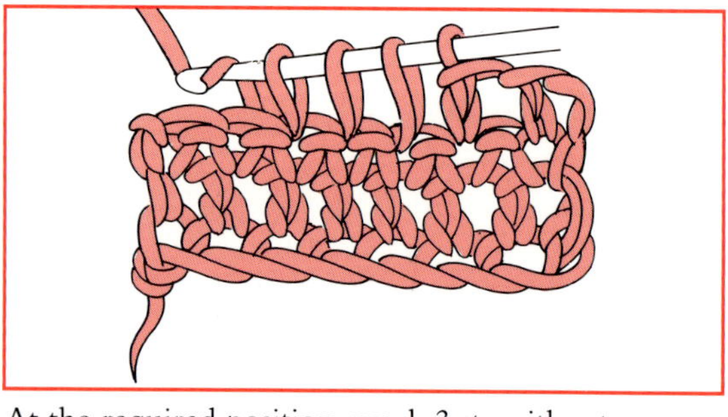

At the required position, work 3 sts without

completing them, leaving 4 loops on hook, yrh and draw through all the loops together.

Working in Rounds

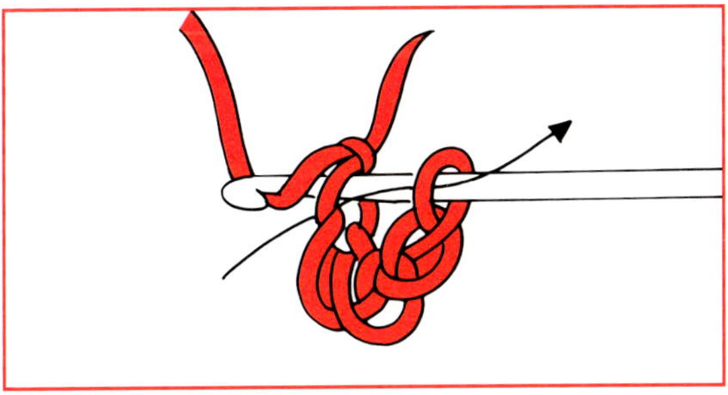

1 To start, make 3 or more ch, then work a slip stitch into the first ch, forming a ring.

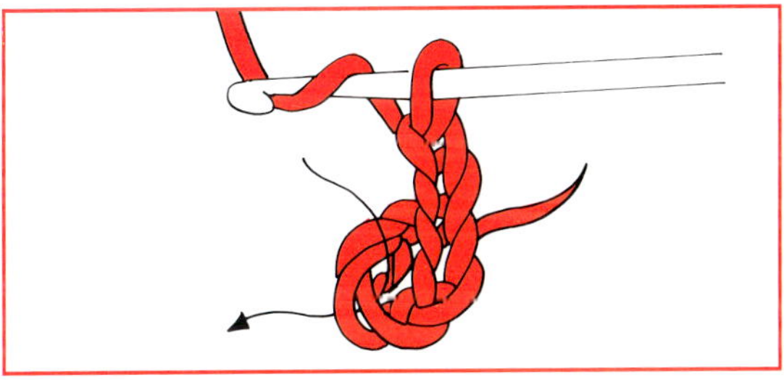

2 To work the first round, make a starting chain to match the height of the stitches to be worked. This serves the same purpose as the turning chain described on page 27. The chart on the same page gives the number of chain required for different stitches.

3 Next insert the hook into the centre of the chain ring to work the sts of the first round.

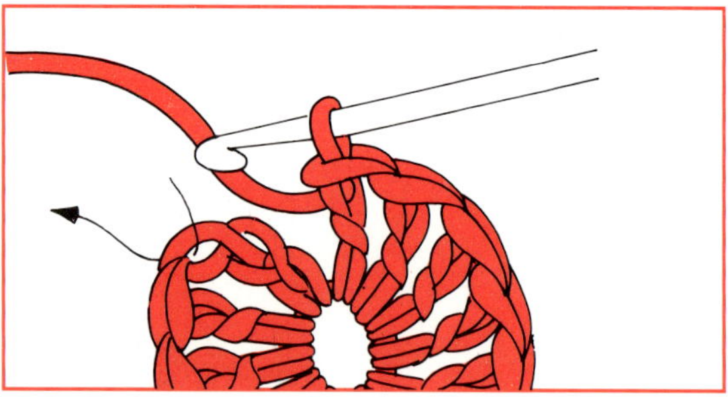

4 At the end of the round, work a ss into the top of the starting ch at the beginning of the round.

5 To work subsequent rounds, begin with a starting chain as before but work the stitches into the top of the stitches in the previous row. Finish each round with a ss as before.

Working in spirals

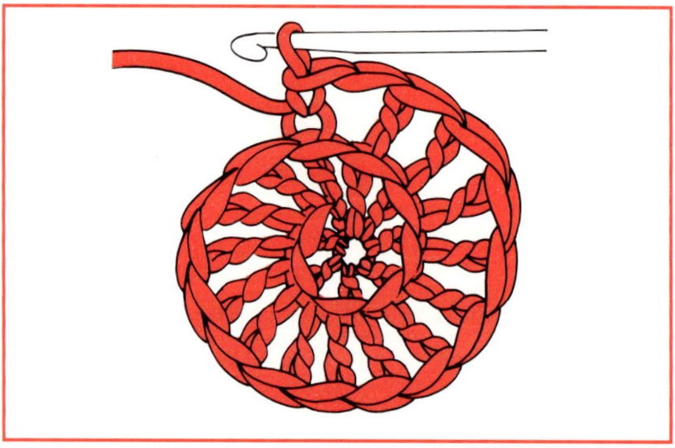

Make the central ring as above and work the first round in the same way but do not finish with a slip stitch, just keep on going for the second round, which will create a spiral.

Working an oval in double crochet

Make a base chain. The length of this chain determines the shape of the oval. For the first round, work dc as normal into the base ch. At the end of the ch, work 3 dc into the last st, turn the work and crochet dc into the opposite side of each st of the base ch. At the end of this round, work 2 dc into the last st.

To complete the round, either work a slip stitch to close the round, or continue working dc to produce a spiral pattern. Continue in this way working through both loops of the stitch below after the first round.

Following a Pattern

Most crochet patterns are produced by yarn manufacturers or appear in magazines. They give you all the information you need to produce a garment that looks like the illustration. The information is usually presented in a logical form that is easy to follow.

Materials are usually listed in the first paragraph that appears on the pattern. The list includes how much yarn you need, what size hooks to use and whether you need buttons, etc.

Measurements are very important as they tell you what the finished size of the garment will be. Compare the "actual" measurements with the "to fit" measurements as the amount of ease given can vary from style to style. You may want to make a size smaller or larger than the size to fit you, if you do not feel happy with the amount of ease allowed.

A pattern will usually be written to suit three or four different sizes. Any variation in the number of stitches required will be given in brackets, e.g. an instruction might read: "to suit sizes 10 (12, 14) work a base chain of 20 (30, 40) stitches." Once you have decided which size is for you, go through the pattern and mark all the instructions related to your size so that it is easier to read.

Tension is the most important part of producing a perfect garment. The tension stated in the pattern is the one obtained by the designer, using the quoted yarn and hook size, and therefore used to design the garment and produce the stated measurements.

Making and measuring a tension swatch

To check that your tension matches the one given in the instructions, make a sample swatch, using the yarn, hook and stitches stated in the pattern. Work in solid rows. The tension is usually given over 4in(10cm), but make a swatch at least 6in(15cm) square. Place the sample on a padded surface and gently smooth it into shape without distorting the stitches. Pin the corners and sides inserting the pins at right angles to the fabric. The tension of both the stitches across the rows and the rows themselves needs to be checked.

For the stitch tension, use pins as markers and count the number of stitches recommended in the tension given. Using a rigid ruler measure the distance between the pins. If your tension is correct, it should measure 4in(10cm).

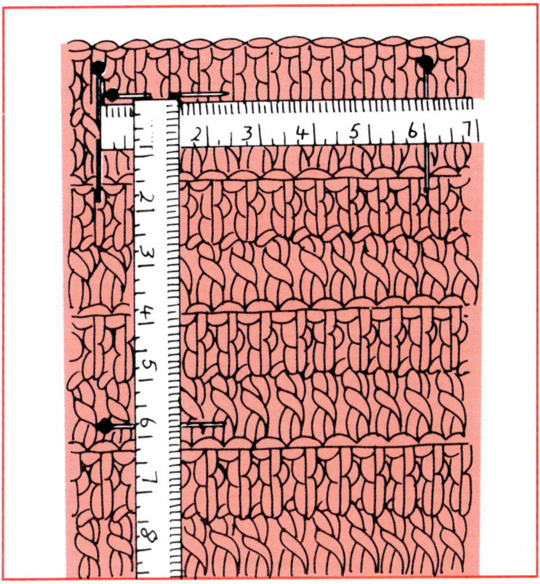

If you have fewer stitches than stated this means your crochet is too loose; if you have more stitches than stated, your crochet is too tight. If your tension is too loose make another swatch using a smaller hook. If your tension is too tight make another swatch using a larger hook.

Your tension must be accurate, even if it is only one stitch out, it could make the finished garment too big or too small. It is well worth spending the time before you start on the actual pattern to get it right.

For the row tension, follow the same procedure as for the stitch tension. If your stitch tension is accurate but your row tension is slightly out, this should not make much difference to most garments.

Abbreviations

Abbreviations are used in crochet patterns to keep the instructions short and precise. If every word was written in long hand, each pattern would make a small book. The following abbreviations are the ones most commonly used.

alt - alternate
beg - beginning
bl(s) - block(s) (in "filet crochet")
ch - chain
cm - centimetres
cont - continue
dc - double crochet
dec - decrease or decreasing
foll - following
htr - half treble
in - inches
inc - increase or increasing
LH - lefthand
lp(s) - loop(s)
MB - make bobble (exact instructions will be given in the individual pattern for the type and size of bobble required)
mm - millimetres
patt - pattern
quadtr - quadruple treble
quintr - quintuple treble
rem - remain or remaining
rep - repeat
RH - righthand
rnd(s) - round(s)
RS - right side
sp(s) - space(s) (in "filet crochet")
ss - slip stitch

st(s) - stitch(es)
tog - together
tr - treble
tr tr - triple treble
WS - wrong side
yrh - yarn round hook

Crochet symbols

Some patterns give instructions by way of symbols. Once you are familiar with the symbols you may well find them easier to follow than written instructions.

The chart on the following two pages shows the main symbols used, although some patterns may have slight variations on these. A pattern will usually have a key to the symbols used.

SYMBOL	MEANING
	chain
	slip stitch
	double crochet
	half treble
	treble
	double treble
	triple treble
	quadruple treble
	two treble worked into one stitch
	three treble worked into one stitch
	four treble worked into one stitch

SYMBOL	MEANING
	picot of three chain
	two loop popcorn
	three loop popcorn
	four loop popcorn
	two loop puff stitch
	three loop puff stitch
	four loop puff stitch
	two loop cluster
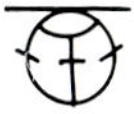	three loop cluster
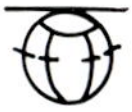	four loop cluster

Written instructions

These are the main part of the pattern and tell you how to make a garment from beginning to end. The instructions are grouped under headings which are usually in a bold type so they are easily spotted when reading the instructions.

Asterisks

An asterisk (*) is a common symbol in crochet instructions. It is used to save the same instruction being given over and over again, for example:
* 1 ch, 1 tr in next tr; rep from * to end of row means you just keep working 1 ch, 1 tr in next tr, until the last stitch has been worked.

Square brackets

Another space saving technique is to put instructions that are to repeated in square brackets [ ] and then state how many times this set of instructions is to be repeated, for example:
[1 ch, 1 tr in next tr] 4 times.

Measuring

This is a most important part of producing a well fitting garment. Lay the piece of crochet on a flat surface. Using a rigid ruler, take all measurements on the straight, never measure round curves.

Blocking

This is the term used for pinning and pressing. Most crochet does not need pressing, but if it is necessary follow the instructions carefully.
Prepare a padded surface - a blanket on a table and

covered with a clean cloth will suffice. Lay the crocheted piece on top, wrong side up and smooth it out to the correct measurements. Check that the rows and edges are running straight. Place pins through the edge at right angles to it, at frequent intervals to obtain a smooth line. Do not pin or press any rib sections.

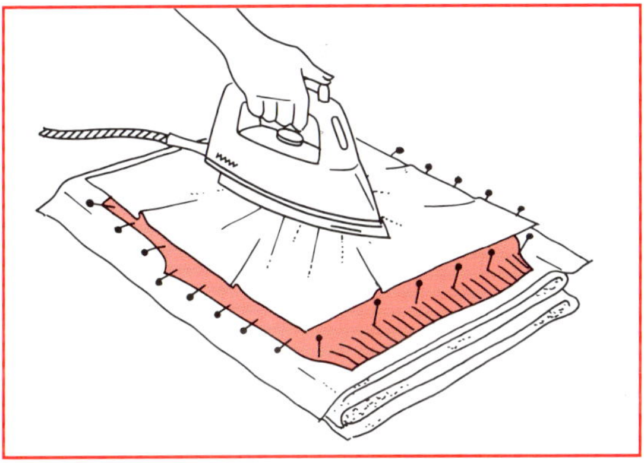

Follow the pressing instructions given on the printed ball-band of the yarn you are using (see page 10). Take a pressing cloth, wet or dry, place over the crochet and with the iron set at the correct temperature, move the iron from section to section by lifting it up and placing it down - do not use an ironing movement as this could distort the stitches. Leave the crochet to dry completely before removing the pins.

Making up

Making up the garment should be done with great care. A beautifully crocheted garment can be spoilt by bad making up. It cannot be rushed.

Sewing up

This can be done using a variety of stitches, depending on what sort of edges are to be sewn together. Generally, you should use the same yarn for making up that the garment was crocheted with. For thick yarns it may be possible to split the yarn to make thinner strands. For a textured yarn, use a matching smooth yarn.

Backstitch seams

These are strong and give a firm seam, they are mainly used on cast-off edges and side seams.

1 With right sides together, pin the seam together. Using a blunt-ended needle, make a double stitch to begin with.

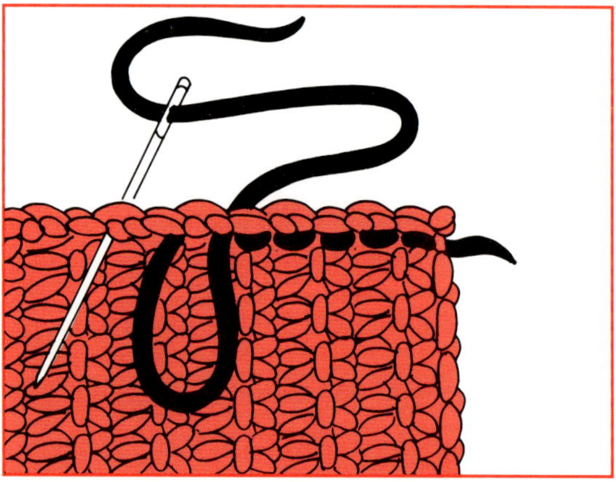

2 Make a running stitch no more than 3/8in(1cm) long and push the needle through the fabric from the back to the front, pull the thread through. Take a backward stitch, inserting the needle at the end of the last stitch, bring the needle through the fabric from back to front a further 3/8 in(1cm) on. Pull the thread through. Continue in this way to the end of the seam. Finish with a double stitch. Loose ends can be darned into the seam or through the centre of the stitches.

Part 3:
PATTERNS

Motifs

Most motifs are worked in rounds from the centre outward. They are worked in continuous rounds with the right side facing. Most motifs start with a length of chain which is joined into a circle. The first round is worked into the circle. The shape of the motif is determined by the type and frequency of the increases.

Square motifs will have 4 lots of increases all worked on top of each other.

Pentagonal motifs will have 5 lots of increases, evenly spaced around the motif, all worked on top of each other.

Circular motifs have increases on every row, worked between the increases on the previous row, to produce a smooth circle rather than a shape with corners. Plain yarns are the best to use as they will show the stitches to their best effect.

Simple "granny" square

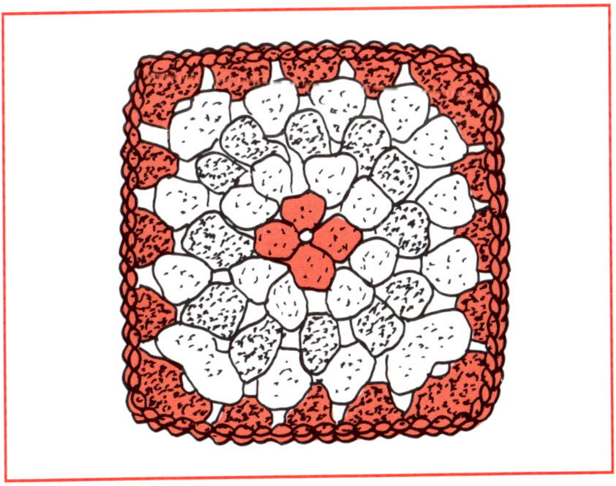

These instructions make a square motif formed from groups of trebles. Motifs can be joined in various ways as described on page 59.
It is worked in five colours: A, B, C, D and E.
Using A, make 6 ch, ss into 1st ch to form a ring.

Round 1 3 ch, into ring work 2 tr, [1 ch, 3 tr] 3 times, 1 ch, ss into top of 3 ch. Fasten off.

Round 2 Join B to any of the 1 ch spaces and work 3 ch, into same sp work [2 tr, 1 ch, 3 tr], ⋆ 1 ch, in next ch sp work [3 tr, 1 ch, 3 tr]; rep from ⋆ twice more, 1 ch, ss in top of 3 ch. Fasten off.

Round 3 Join C to any of the corner spaces and work 3 ch, into same sp work [2 tr, 1 ch, 3 tr], ⋆ 1 ch, 3 tr in next ch sp, 1 ch, in next ch sp work [3 tr, 1 ch, 3 tr]; rep from ⋆ twice more, 1 ch, 3 tr in next ch sp, 1 ch, ss in top of 3 ch. Fasten off.

Round 4 Join D to any of the corner spaces and work 3 ch, into same sp work [2 tr, 1 ch, 3 tr], ⋆ [1 ch, 3 tr in next ch sp] twice, 1 ch, in next ch sp work [3 tr, 1 ch, 3 tr]; rep from ⋆ twice more, [1 ch, 3 tr in next ch sp] twice, 1 ch, ss in top of 3 ch. Fasten off.

Round 5 Join E to any of the corner spaces and work 3 ch, into same sp work [2 tr, 1 ch, 3 tr], ⋆ [1 ch, 3 tr in next ch sp] 3 times, 1 ch, in next ch sp work [3 tr, 1 ch, 3 tr]; rep from ⋆ twice more, [1 ch, 3 tr in next ch sp] 3 times, 1 ch, ss in top of 3 ch. Fasten off.
Continue in this way until the square is the required size.

Simple "granny" pentagon

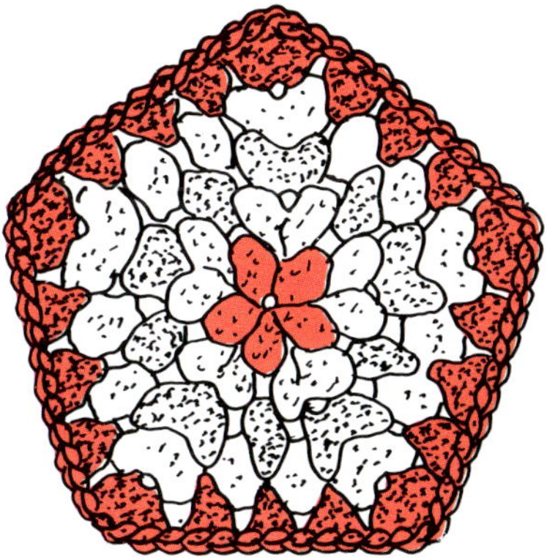

Worked in five colours: A, B, C, D and E.
Using A make 4 ch, ss in 1st ch to form a ring.

Round 1 3 ch, into ring work 1 tr, [1 ch, 2 tr] 4times, 1 ch, ss into top of 3 ch. Fasten off.

Round 2 Join B to any of the 1 ch spaces and work 3 ch, into same sp work [1 tr, 1 ch, 2 tr], * 1 ch, in next ch sp work [2 tr, 1 ch, 2 tr]; rep from * 3 times more, 1 ch, ss in top of 3 ch. Fasten off.

Round 3 Join C to any of the 1 ch spaces and work 3 ch, into same sp work [1 tr, 1 ch, 2 tr], * 1 ch, 2 tr in next ch sp, 1 ch, in next ch sp work [2 tr, 1 ch, 2 tr]; rep from * 3 times more, 1 ch, 2 tr in next ch sp, 1 ch, ss in top of 3 ch. Fasten off.

Round 4 Join D to any of the corner spaces and work 3 ch, into same sp work [1 tr, 1 ch, 2 tr], * [1 ch, 2 tr in next ch sp] twice, 1 ch, in next ch sp work [2 tr, 1 ch, 2 tr]; rep from ⋆ 3 times more, [1 ch, 2 tr in next ch sp] twice, 1 ch, ss in top of 3 ch. Fasten off.

Round 5 Join E to any of the corner spaces and work 3 ch, into same sp work [1 tr, 1 ch, 2 tr], ⋆ [1 ch, 2 tr in next ch sp] 3 times, 1 ch, in next ch sp work [2 tr, 1 ch, 2 tr]; rep from ⋆ 3 times more, [1 ch, 2 tr in next ch sp] 3 times, 1 ch, ss in top of 3 ch. Fasten off.
Continue in this way until the pentagon is the required size.

Simple "granny" hexagon

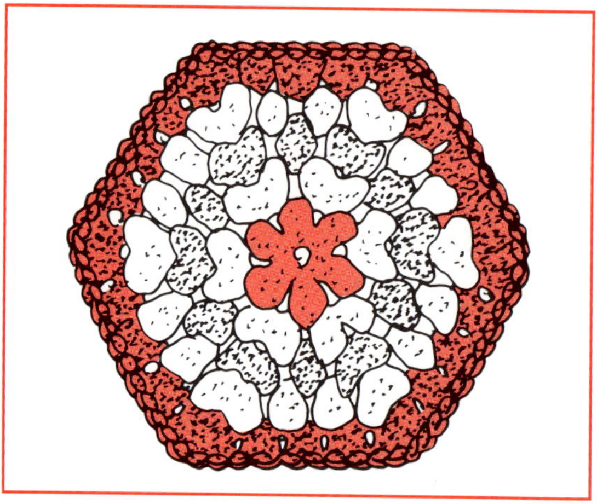

Worked in five colours: A, B, C, D and E.
Using A make 6 ch, ss in 1st ch to form a ring.

Round 1 3 ch, into ring work 1 tr, [1 ch, 2 tr] 5 times, 1 ch, ss into top of 3 ch. Fasten off.

Round 2 Join B to any of the 1 ch spaces and work 3 ch, into same sp work [1 tr, 1 ch, 2 tr], ⋆ 1 ch, in next ch sp work [2 tr, 1 ch, 2 tr]; rep from ⋆ 4 times more, 1 ch, ss in top of 3 ch. Fasten off.

Round 3 Join C to any of the 1 ch spaces and work 3 ch, into same sp work [1 tr, 1 ch, 2 tr], ⋆ 1 ch, 2 tr in next ch sp, 1 ch, in next ch sp work [2 tr, 1 ch, 2 tr]; rep from ⋆ 4 times more, 1 ch, 2 tr in next ch sp, 1 ch, ss in top of 3 ch. Fasten off.

Round 4 Join D to any of the corner spaces and work 3 ch, into same sp work [1 tr, 1 ch, 2 tr], ⋆ [1 ch, 2 tr in next ch sp] twice, 1 ch, in next ch sp work [2 tr, 1 ch, 2 tr]; rep from ⋆ 4 times more, [1 ch, 2 tr in next ch sp] twice, 1 ch, ss in top of 3 ch. Fasten off.

Round 5 Join E to any of the corner spaces and work 3 ch, into same sp work [1 tr, 1 ch, 2 tr], ⋆ [1 ch, 2 tr in next ch sp] 3 times, 1 ch, in next ch sp work [2 tr, 1 ch, 2 tr]; rep from ⋆ 4 times more, [1 ch, 2 tr in next ch sp] 3 times, 1 ch, ss in top of 3 ch. Fasten off.
Continue in this way until the hexagon is the required size.

Simple "granny" octagon

Worked in five colours: A, B, C, D and E.
Using A make 6 ch, ss in 1st ch to form a ring.

Round 1 3 ch, into ring work 2 tr, [1 ch, 3 tr] 3 times, 1 ch, ss into top of 3 ch. Fasten off.

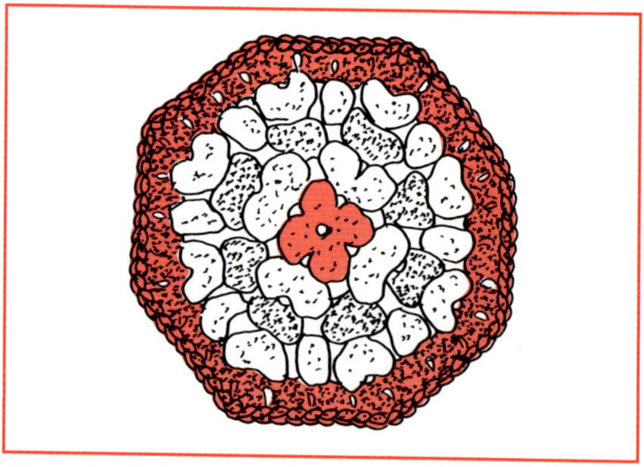

Round 2 Join B to any of the 1 ch spaces and work 3 ch, into same sp work [2 tr, 1 ch, 3 tr], * 1 ch, in next ch sp work [3 tr, 1 ch, 3 tr]; rep from * twice more, 1 ch, ss in top of 3 ch. Fasten off.

Round 3 Join C to next 1 ch space and work 3 ch, into same sp work [1 tr, 1 ch, 2 tr], * 1 ch, in next ch sp work [2 tr, 1 ch, 2 tr]; rep from * 6 times more, 1 ch, ss in top of 3 ch. Fasten off.

Round 4 Join D to any of the corner spaces and work 3 ch, into same sp work [1 tr, 1 ch, 2 tr], * 1 ch, 2 tr in next ch sp, in next ch sp work [2 tr, 1 ch, 2 tr]; rep from * 6 times more, 1 ch, 2 tr in next ch sp, 1 ch, ss in top of 3 ch. Fasten off.

Round 5 Join E to any of the corner spaces and work 3 ch, into same sp work [1 tr, 1 ch, 2 tr], * [1 ch, 2 tr in next ch sp] twice, 1 ch, in next ch sp work [2 tr, 1 ch, 2 tr]; rep from * 6 times more, [1 ch, 2 tr in next ch sp] twice, 1 ch, ss in top of 3 ch. Fasten off.
Continue in this way until the required size.

Joining motifs

Depending on their shape, some motifs (such as squares and hexagons) fit together exactly. There are various methods of joining them, depending on personal preference.

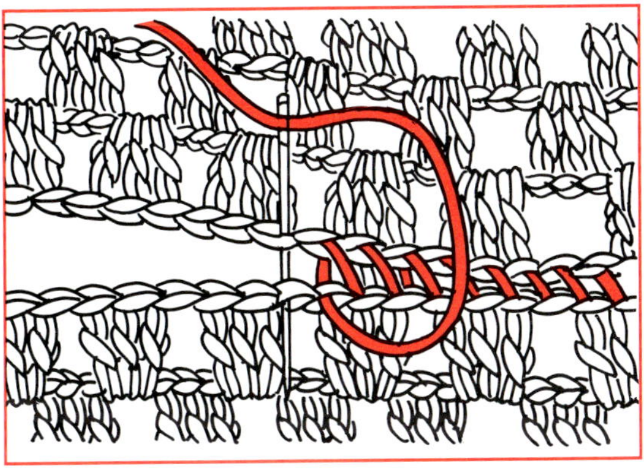

1 With a flat seam, using a blunt-ended needle and matching yarn.

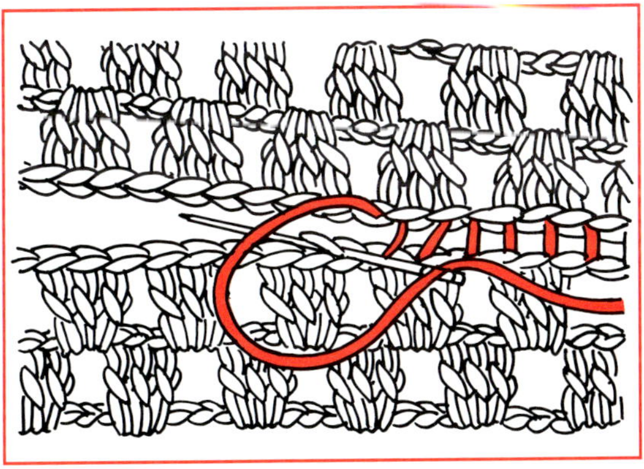

2 By weaving, using a blunt-ended needle and matching yarn.

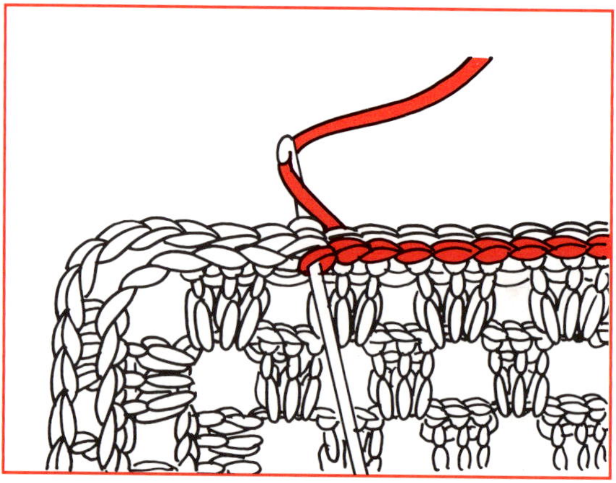

3 By slip stitch, using a crochet hook and matching yarn.

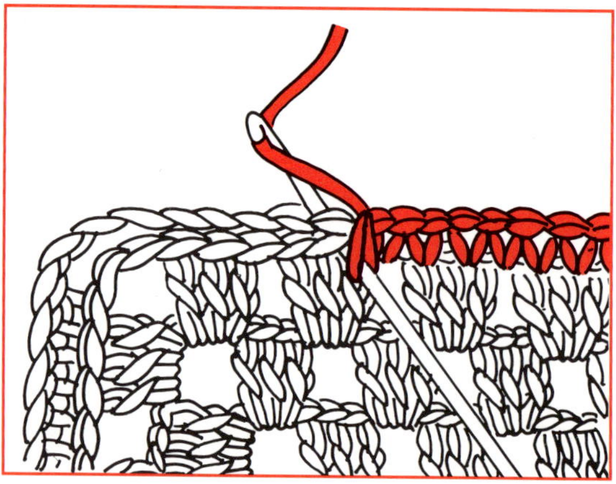

4 By double crochet, using a crochet hook and matching yarn.

5 By crab stitch (see below), using a crochet hook and matching or contrasting yarn, worked on the right side of the motifs.

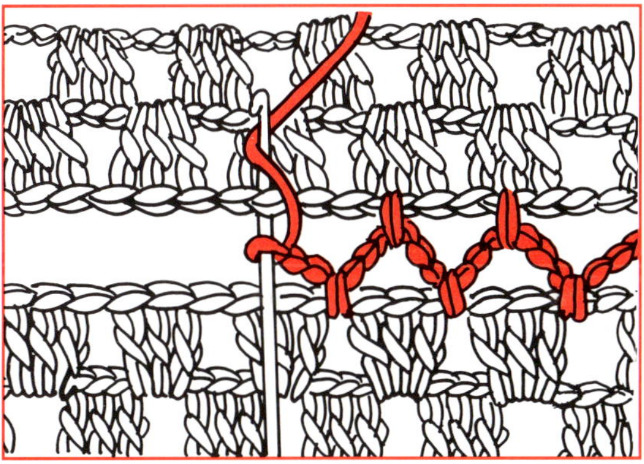

6 Fancy or openwork motifs may be joined with a series of chain stitches, anchored with a slip stitch or double crochet.

Crab stitch

This is double crochet worked from left to right and is ideal for giving row-ends a finished look. Work a row of dc, do not turn the work, then work as follows:

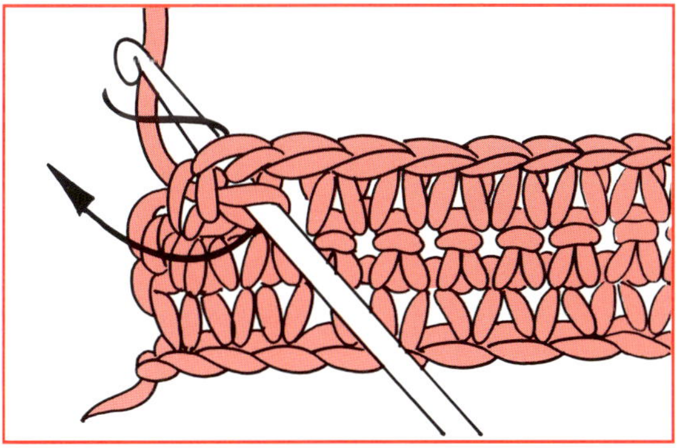

1 With the hook facing downwards, insert it into

the next st to the right, pull the yarn through, twisting the hook to face upwards at the same time (2 lps on hook).

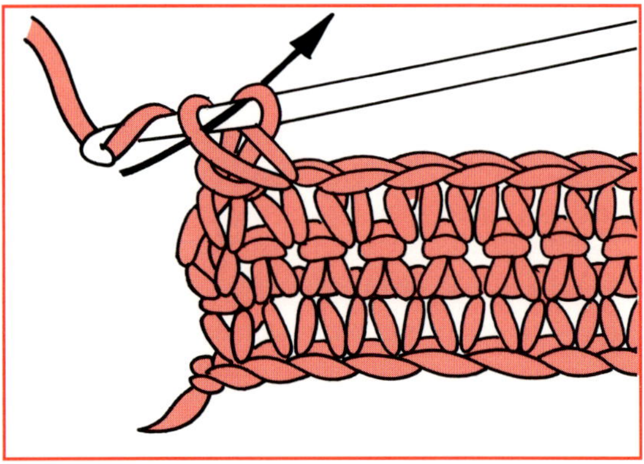

2 Yrh and draw through both lps to finish the dc.

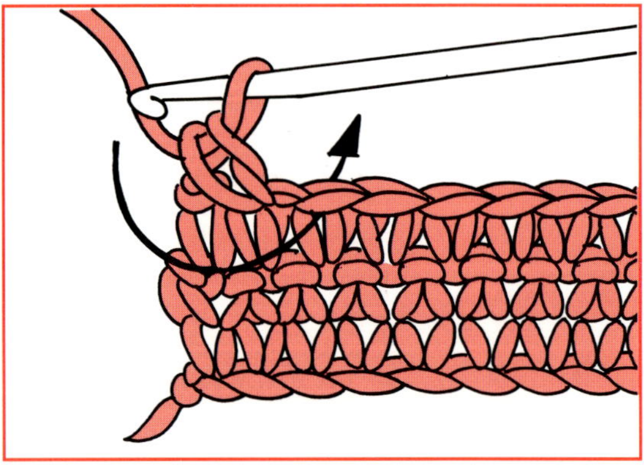

3 Insert the hook into the next stitch as before and repeat to end of row.

The direction of the work causes the stitches to twist and create a corded effect.

Filet Crochet

Filet crochet is mainly worked in cotton and the designs are used for making curtains, edgings for shelves, tablecloths and collars. The designs are worked as a mesh, by filling in some squares and leaving other squares open. These designs are nearly always worked from a chart in the form of a graph. The designs can be geometric or representational.

Working a simple mesh

Make the required number of chain in a multiple of 3 plus 5 extra.

Foundation row: work 1 tr into 8th ch from hook. ⋆ miss 2 ch, 1 tr in next ch; rep from ⋆ to end.

Next row: 5 ch (to count as first tr and 2 ch space), 1 tr in next tr, ⋆ 2 ch, 1 tr in next tr; rep from ⋆ to end, working last tr in 3rd of 8 ch.

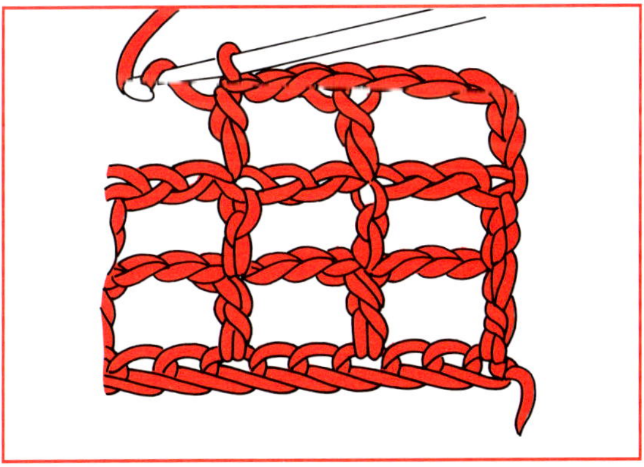

Subsequent rows: 5 ch, 1 tr in next tr, ⋆ 2 ch, 1 tr

in next tr; rep from * to end, working last tr in 3rd of 5 ch.

Working a foundation row of open squares

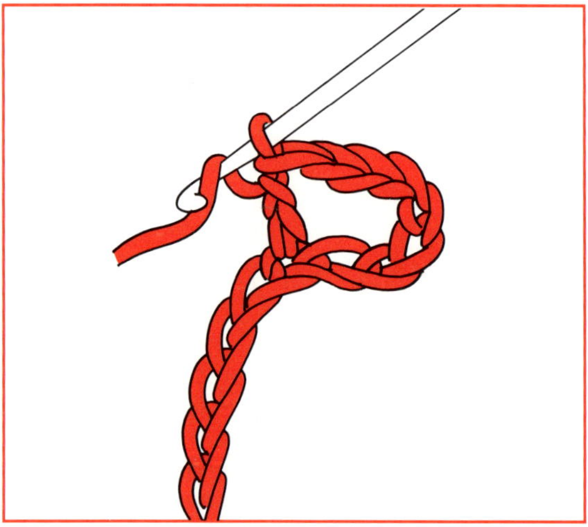

To start the foundation row with an open square, work 1 tr into 8th ch from hook. For every subsequent open square work 2 ch, miss 2 ch on base row, 1 tr in next ch. An open square is made up of a 2 ch sp with 1 tr on either side of it.

Working a foundation row of filled squares

To start the foundation row with a filled square, work 1 tr into 4th ch from hook, then 1 tr into each of next 2 ch. For every subsequent filled square work 1 tr into each of next 3 tr. A filled

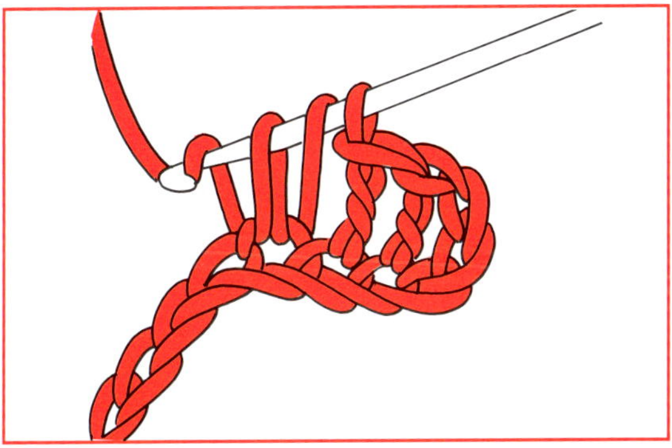

square is made up of 2 tr instead of a 2 ch sp with 1 tr on either side of it.

Working filled squares at the beginning of a row

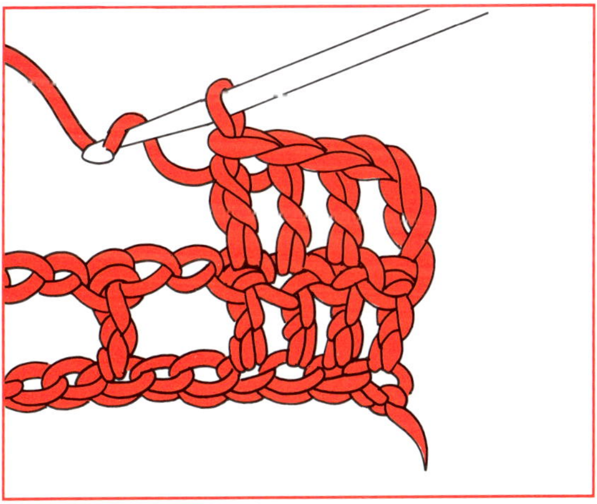

At the beginning of the row work 3 ch to count as first tr. Now work 2 tr over either 2 tr or 2 ch sp, then work 1 tr in next tr.

Working open squares at the beginning of a row

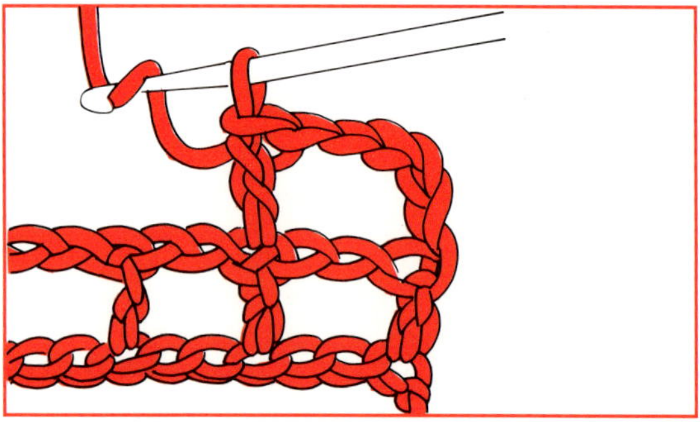

At the beginning of the row make 5 ch, to count as first tr and 2 ch sp. Miss either the next 2 tr or 2 ch sp on previous row, then work 1 tr in next tr.

Working more than one filled square together

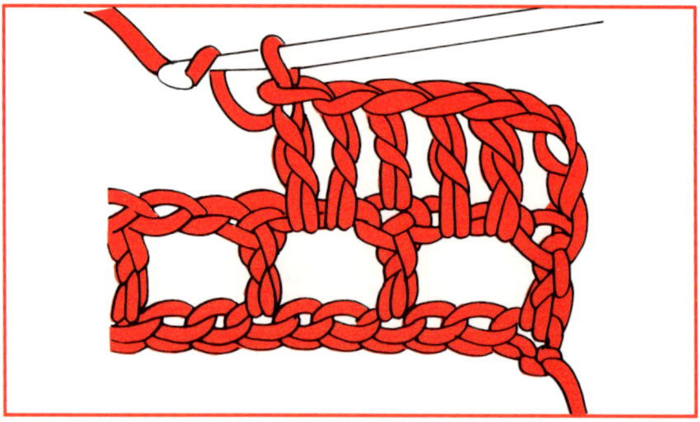

After working a filled square at the beginning of the row, only 3 tr are required for each subsequent filled square - 2 tr over the central 2 ch sp, then 1 tr to complete the square.

Increasing by one open square at the beginning of a row

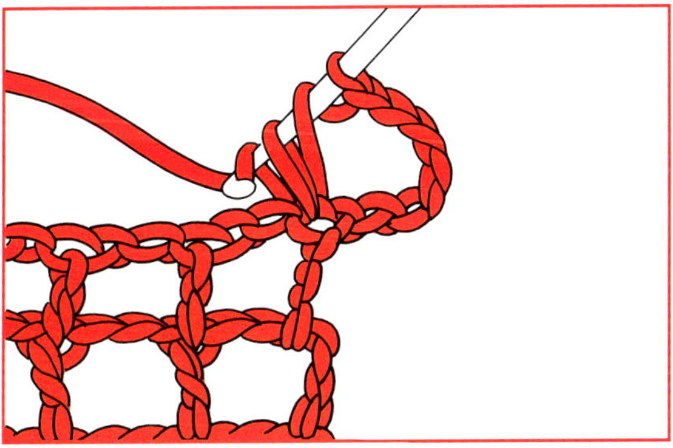

At the end of the previous row make 7 ch, then turn. Work 1 tr in first tr, then continue in pattern to the end of the row.

Increasing by one square at the end of a row

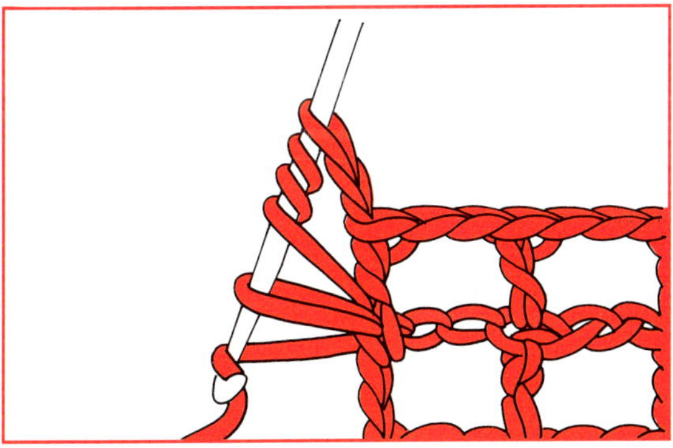

Work in pattern to the end of the row, make 2 ch, then work 1 tr tr into base of last tr of row.

Increasing by more than one open square at the beginning of a row

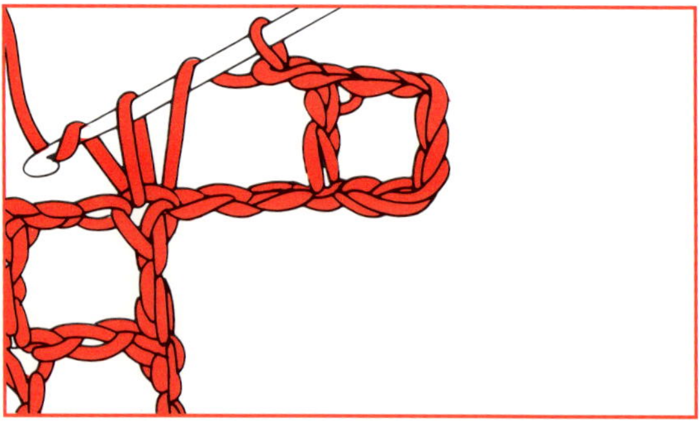

At the end of the previous row, make a length of 3 ch for each open square plus 4 ch. Work 1 tr into 7th ch from hook, then make subsequent squares as follows:

2 ch, miss 2 ch on previous row, 1 tr into next ch.

Increasing by more than one open square at the end of a row

Increase first square at end of row as already given above, then make subsequent squares as follows:

2 ch, 1 tr tr into the corner formed by previous increased square.

Increasing by one filled square at the beginning of a row

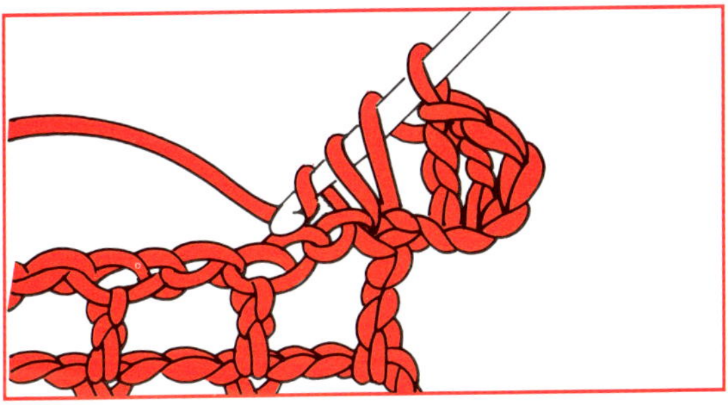

At the end of the previous row make 5 ch, turn, work 1 tr in 4th ch from hook, 1 tr in next ch, then 1 tr in next tr (last tr of previous row), then continue in pattern to end.

Increasing by one filled square at the end of a row

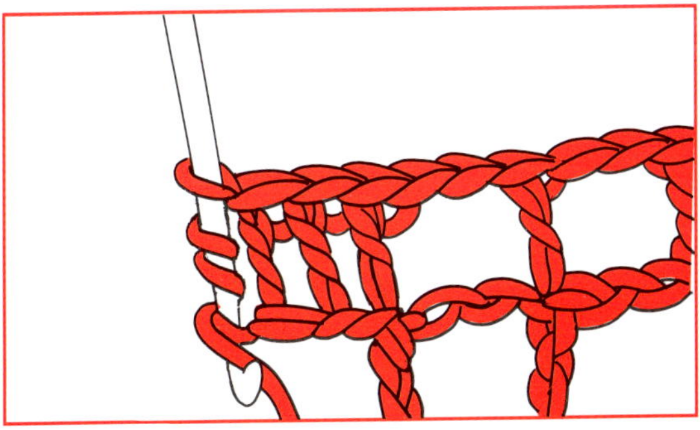

Work in pattern to end of row, then work a dtr into base of last tr of row, [work 1 dtr into base of previous dtr] twice.

Sloped increasing

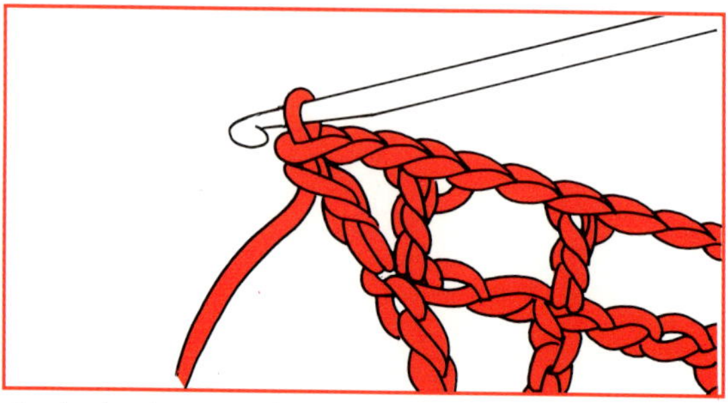

At the beginning of the row work: 5 ch (to count as 1 tr and 2 ch), then 1 tr into first tr. At the end of the row work last tr of row, then work 2 ch, 1 tr in same place as last tr.

Decreasing an open or filled square at the beginning of a row

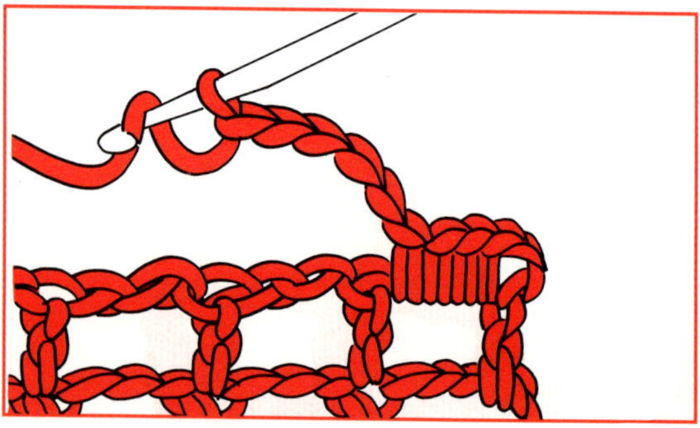

Ss in each of the first 4 sts, make either 3 ch for a filled square or 5 ch for an open square, then pattern to end.

Decreasing an open or filled square at the end of a row

Work in pattern to last square of row, leaving 3 sts unworked, turn, make either 3 ch for a filled square or 5 ch for an open square, then pattern to end.

Sloped decreasing of an open square at the beginning of a row

Make 3 ch instead of 5 then work 1 tr in 2nd tr of row.

Sloped decreasing of an open square at the end of a row

Work to last tr of row, then work 1 tr in 3rd of 5 ch (therefore there are no ch between trebles).

Sloped decreasing of a filled square at the beginning of a row

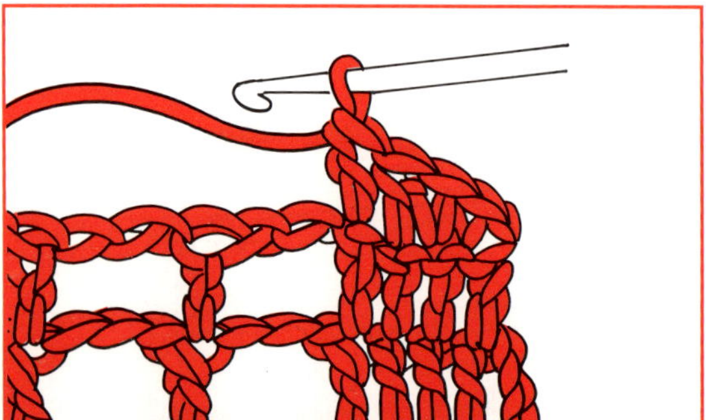

Begin the row by working 1 ss in first tr, 1 dc in next st, 1 htr in next st, then 1 tr in next tr, then pattern to end.

Sloped decreasing of a filled square at the end of a row

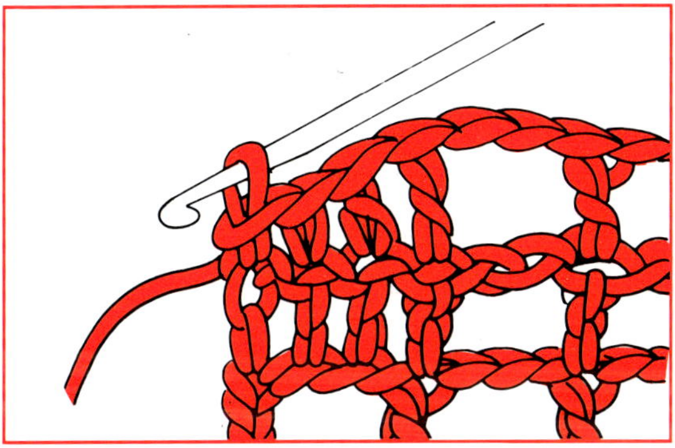

Work to the tr at the end of the first block or space of the previous row, 1 tr in tr, 1htr in next st, 1 dc in next st, 1 ss in last st, turn ss across first 4 sts to start next row.

Working filet crochet from a chart

Charts are read from bottom to top, right side rows from right to left and wrong side rows from left to right. Each open square represents an open space, a filled in square represents a block of stitches. Every row starts with 3 chain - which counts as the first treble - to bring the work to the correct height.

Each open square on the chart represents a space formed by two chain and a treble, the other edge of the open square is formed by the first treble of the next open square or block.

When a square is filled the two chain are replaced by two treble, making a single block of three treble. Each additional block adds three treble. Two blocks together with a space each side appears as seven treble and three blocks as ten treble.

Hairpin Crochet

Hairpin Crochet is more like lace than crochet. Strips of crochet are formed over a hairpin fork, then joined together.

Double crochet strip

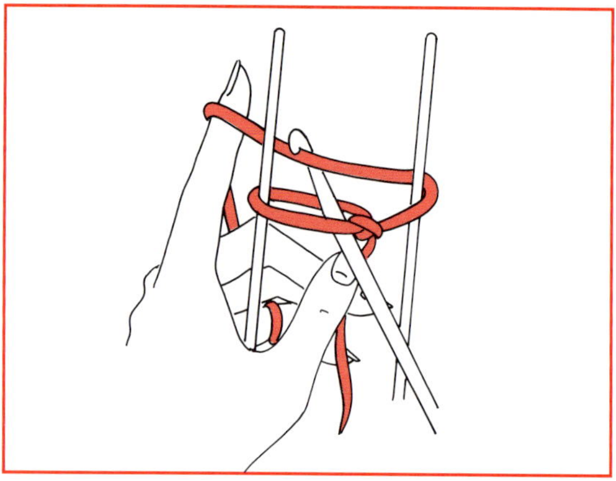

1 Make a slip knot and place the loop on the left prong of the hairpin, so that the knot lies in the centre. Wind the yarn round the right prong from front to back. Insert the hook through the loop and catch the yarn.

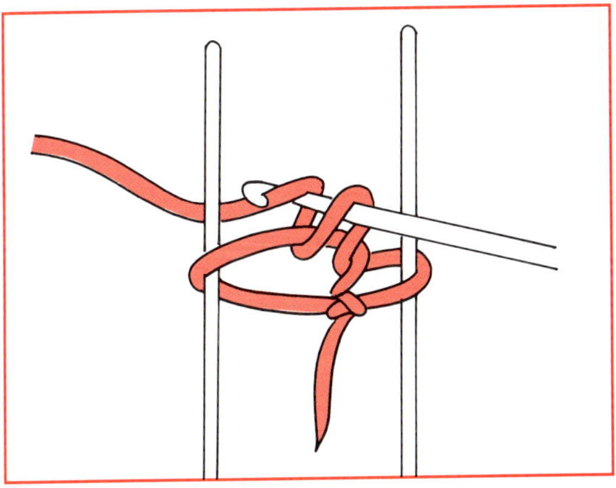

2 Holding the hairpin in the left hand and the hook in the right hand, draw through a loop, yrh, draw through loop on hook to make a stitch on the left loop.

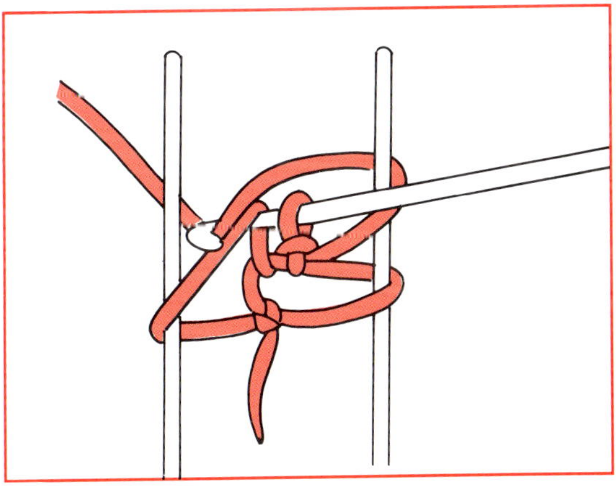

3 * Turn the hairpin to the left, allowing the yarn to wind round the prong of the hairpin as you turn it. Insert the hook under the top loop of the left prong, yrh and draw a loop through.

4 Yrh and draw a loop through both loops on hook *. Rep from * to * until the required number of loop have been worked.

Finishing with double crochet edging

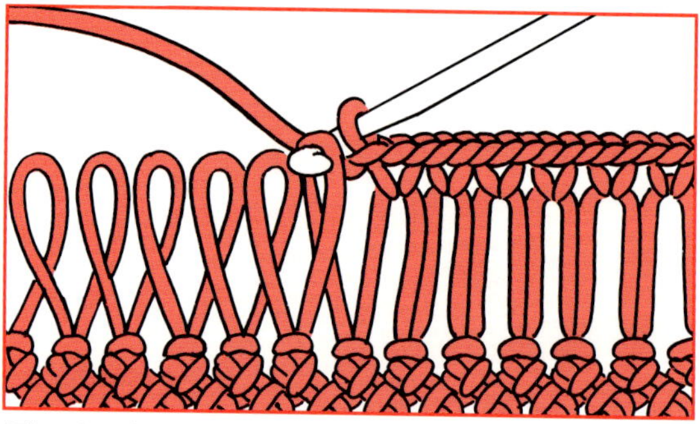

The simplest way to finish a strip of hairpin crochet, whether it is used as a border or insertion is as follows: join the yarn to the first loop at one edge, insert hook into loop and work 1 ch, taking care that the loops are not twisted, work 1 dc in each loop to end. Fasten off.

Finishing with crossed loops

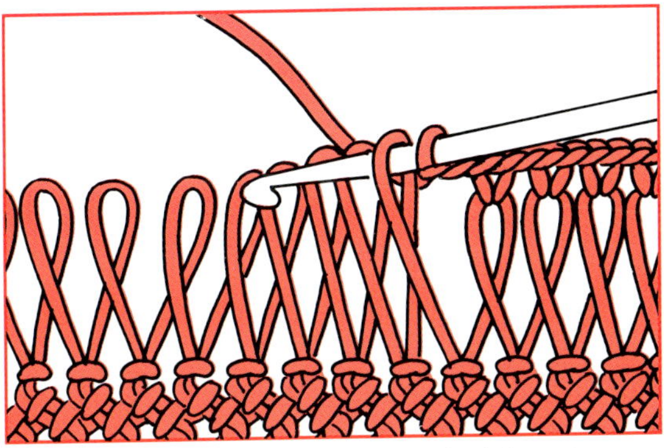

Join yarn to first loop and work 1 ch, * inserting hook from front to back of twisted loop, work 1 dc onto each loop.

Some alternative ways of forming the hairpin crochet strips

Strips made with 2 double crochet

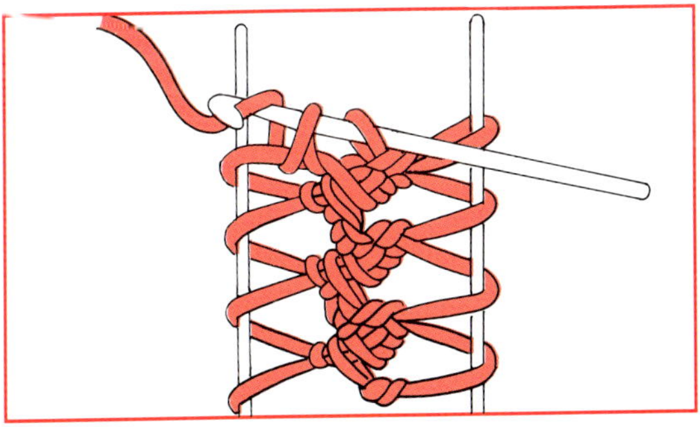

Work as given for double crochet strips, working 2 dc in front of each loop.

Strips made with 3 double crochet

Work as given for double crochet strips, working 3 dc in front of each loop.

Strips made with 1 double crochet and 2 trebles

Work as given for double crochet strips, working 1 dc and 2 tr in front of each loop.

Strips made with double crochet and closed loops

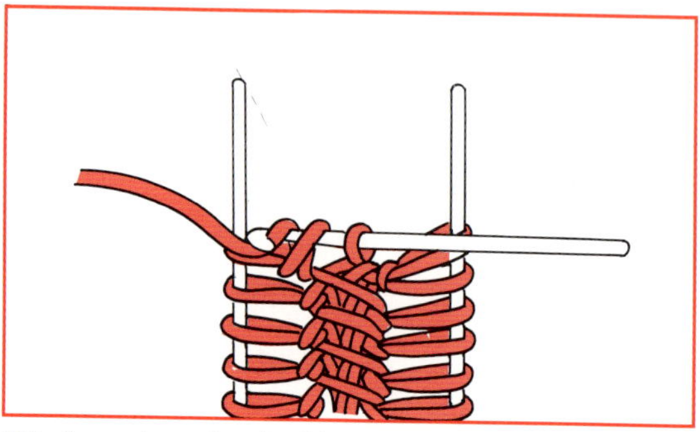

Work as given for double crochet strips, inserting hook below each loop on left prong instead of through it.

Strips made with trebles and closed loops

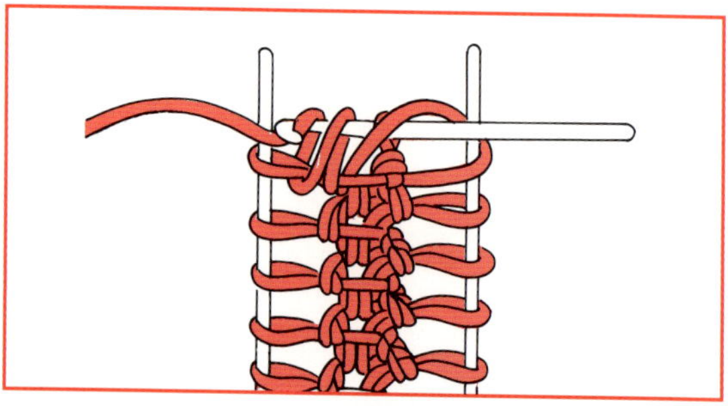

Work as given for double crochet strips, working 1 tr round each loop and inserting hook below each loop on left prong instead of through it.

Working a circular piece of hairpin crochet

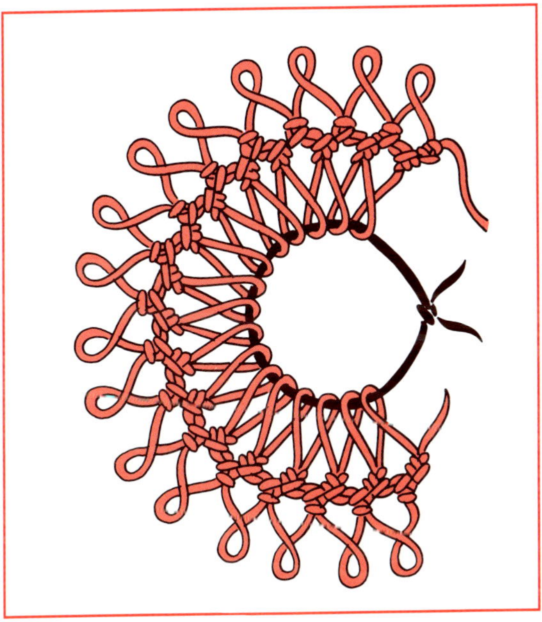

1 Make a strip of hairpin crochet and remove the hairpin, but do not cut off the yarn. Thread a spare length of matching yarn through all loops on one edge, taking care that the loops are all twisted the same way, then draw them up tightly, knot thread and cut.

2 Insert the hook into the last stitch from the last

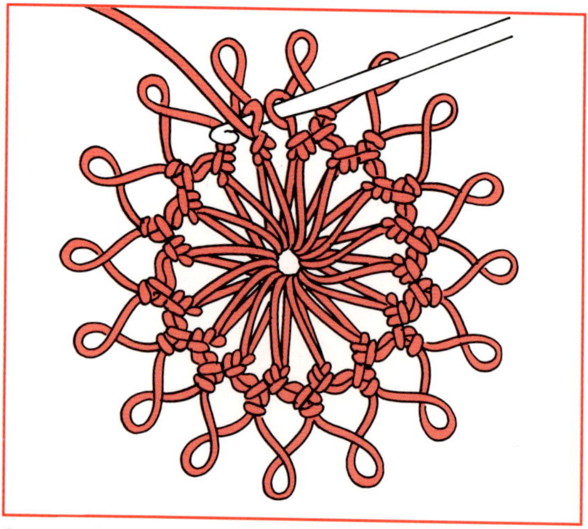

loop and join to the first stitch with a slipstitch. Finish the outer edge by working 1dc into each loop, working 1 or 2 chain between each loop as required.

Joining two strips with chain stitch

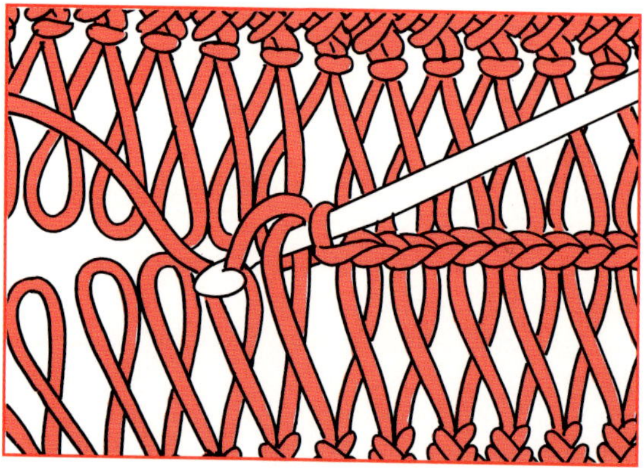

Lay the two strips edge to edge, with right sides facing upwards. Join yarn to first loop in top strip, then insert hook through first loop in bottom strip, yrh and draw through a loop, yrh, and draw through loop on hook, * insert hook through next loop in top strip, then through next loop in bottom strip, yrh and draw through a loop, yrh and draw through loop on hook; rep from * to end.

Peruvian Crochet (also called Broomstick Crochet)

This is worked with one large knitting needle and a crochet hook. Each row is made up of two parts - a forward and a return row, each worked with the right side facing.

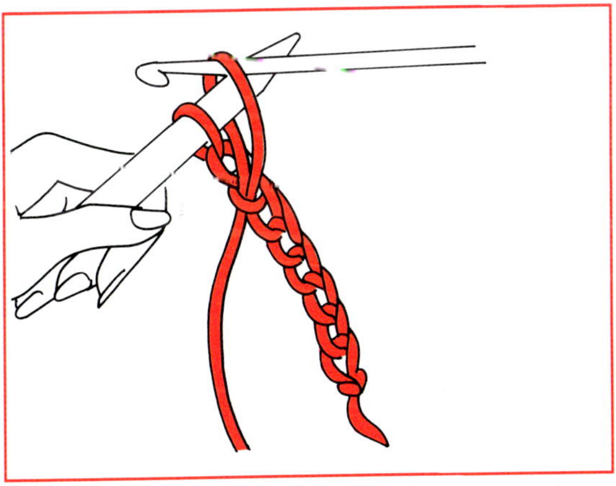

1 Using crochet hook and yarn, commence with the required number of chain, which in this example is divisible by 3. On the forward row begin by placing the first chain loop on the needle, * insert the hook through the next ch, yrh, draw a loop through and place on to the needle.

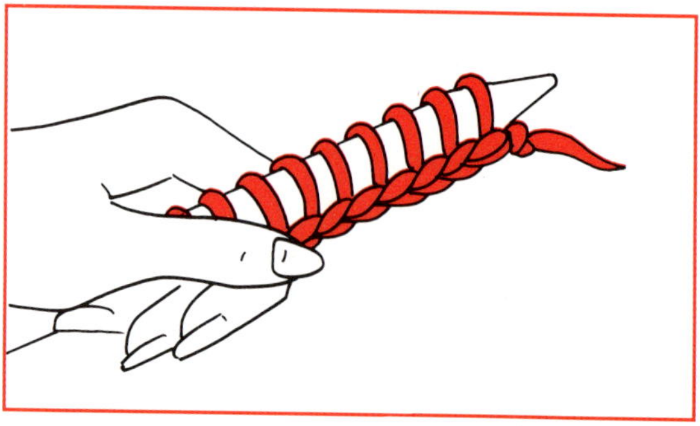

2 Holding the needle in the left hand, rep from * to end of chain, taking care to keep all loops the same length.

Note: this row forms the base row for the work.

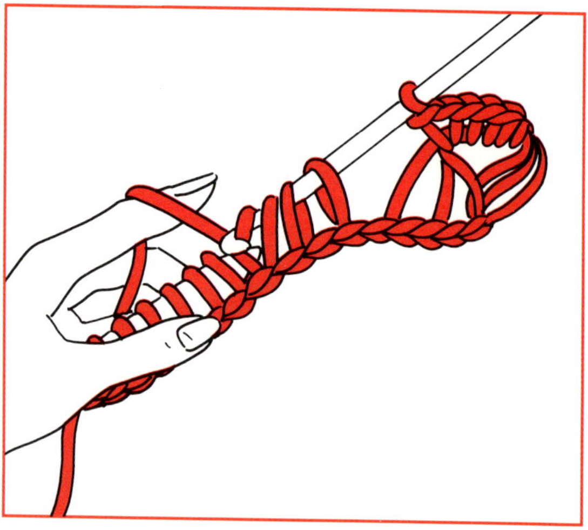

3 Working from right to left and holding the needle

in the left hand and the hook in the right hand, insert the hook through the first 3 loops, taking them off the needle, yrh and draw through a loop, yrh and draw through loop on hook. Now working through all 3 loops again, work 3 dc, ★ inserting hook through the centre of the next 3 loops and taking them off the needle, work 3dc; rep from ★ to end.

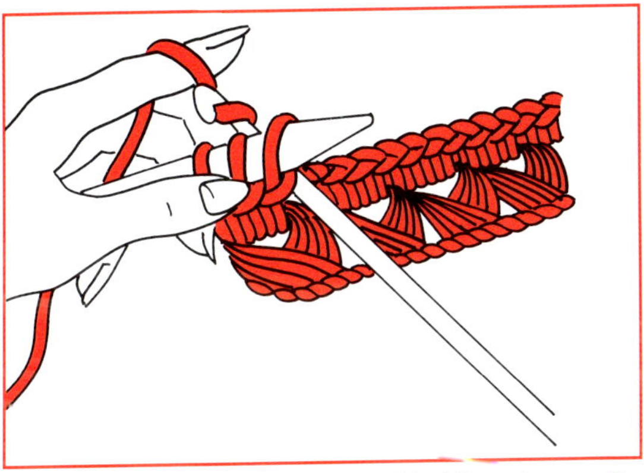

4 Working from left to right and holding the needle in the left hand and the hook in the right hand, insert the hook into the first dc, yrh, draw a loop through and place on the needle, ★ insert the hook in the next dc, yrh, draw a loop through and place on to the needle; rep from ★ to end. Repeat steps 3 and 4 to form the pattern, ending with a row 3

Tunisian Crochet

Tunisian crochet is worked with a special Tunisian crochet hook on a base of chain. It produces a firm fabric rather like a piece of weaving. Each row is formed in two stages without turning the work.

Simple Tunisian stitch

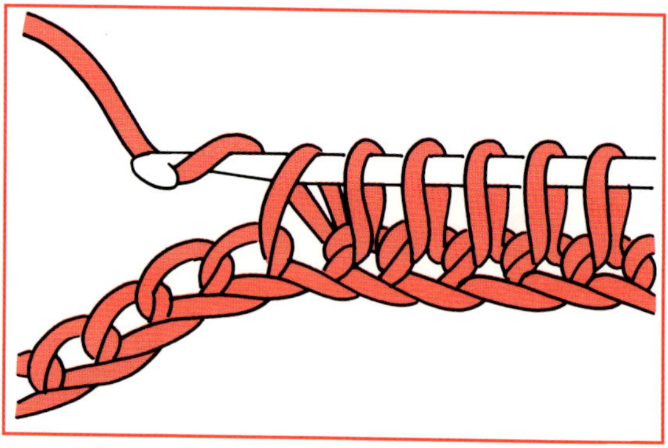

Row 1 (forward) Insert hook into 2nd ch from hook, yrh, draw a loop through and leave on hook, * insert hook through next ch, yrh, draw a loop through and leave on hook; rep from * to end. Do not turn the work.

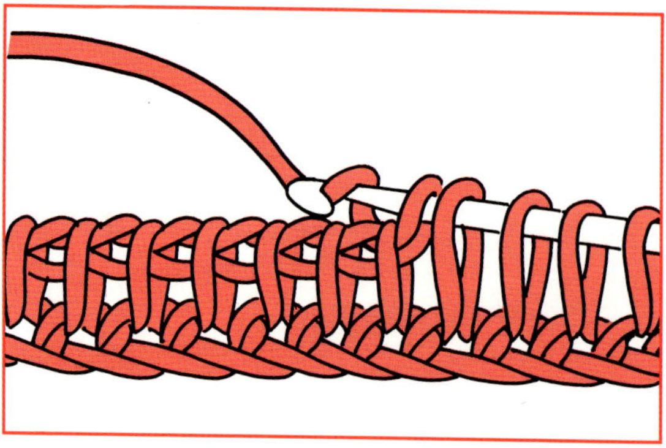

Row 1 (return) Still with the right side of work facing, work yrh, draw through first loop on hook, * yrh, draw through next 2 loops on hook; rep from * to end. This completes the two sections of the first row.

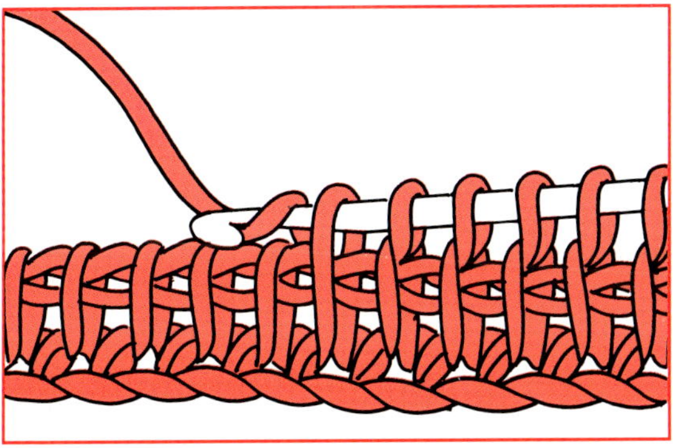

Row 2 (forward) Insert hook from right to left under 2nd vertical loop of last row, yrh, draw a loop through and leave on hook, * insert hook under next loop, yrh, draw a loop through and leave on hook; rep from * to end.

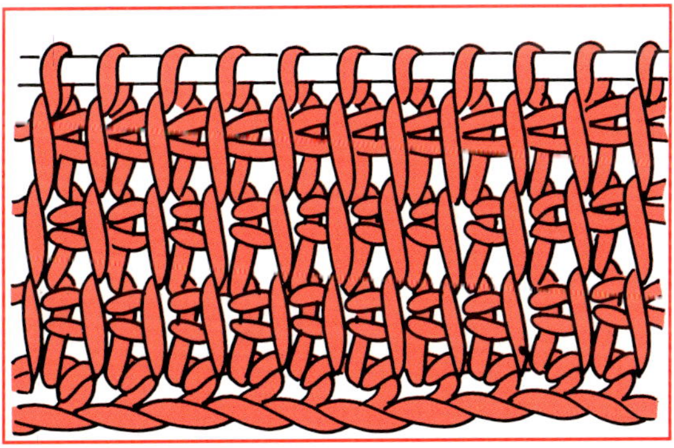

Row 2 (return) As row 1 return. Repeat row 2 forward and return to form the pattern.

Double Tunisian stitch

Make required number of chain and work row 1 as simple Tunisian stitch.

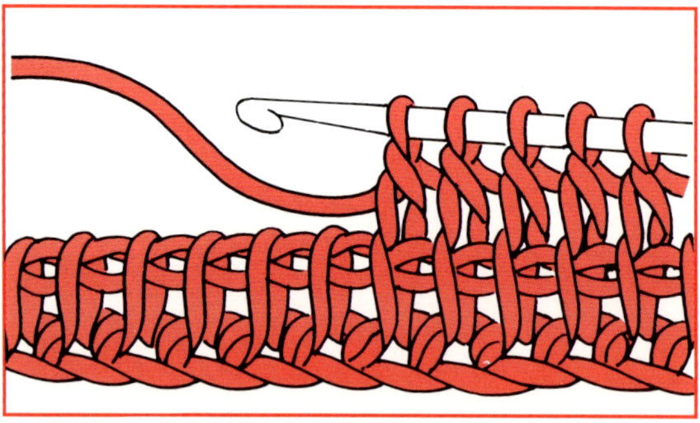

Row 2 (forward) Yrh, draw through loop on hook, * insert hook through next vertical loop of previous row, yrh, draw loop through, yrh, draw through loop on hook leaving a loop on the hook; rep from * to end. Work **return row** as simple Tunisian stitch; rep row 2 to form the pattern.

Finishing the work

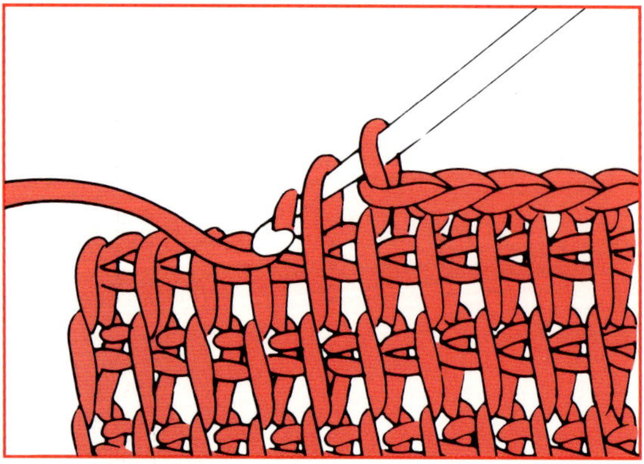

To give a neat edge, work 1 row of dc, inserting the hook under the vertical loop of each stitch but not leaving the loops on the hook.

Part 4:
CARE

CLEANING AND STORING

It is best to clean crocheted garments lightly and often, but with great care. Hand-crocheted garments are not as resilient as ready-made ones - they are more likely to stretch out of shape or shrink if not handled carefully. Unless the printed ball-band of the yarn you are using specifically states that the yarn can be machine washed, it is safest to hand wash or dry clean.

Hand washing

Use a special powder or solution for hand washing delicate fabrics. Completely dissolve the washing agent in warm water, then add sufficient cold water to make it lukewarm.

Immerse the garment in the suds and work quickly, using your hands to expel soapy water by gentle squeezing, never wringing.

Carefully lift the garment out of the water, supporting it with both hands. Rinse the garment in clear

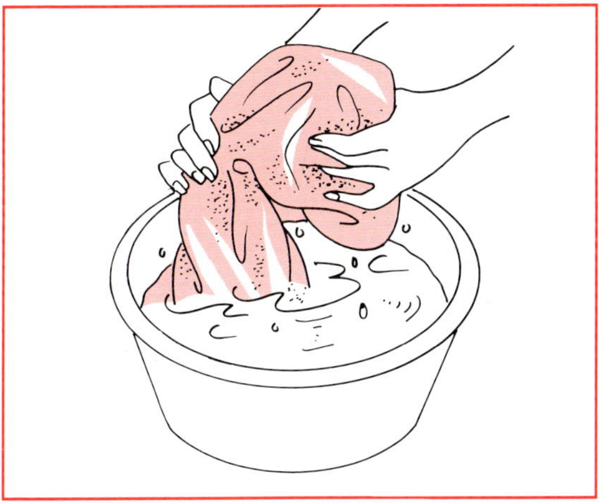

water of the same temperature until the water runs clear. After rinsing, squeeze out as much water as possible, do not wring.

Drying

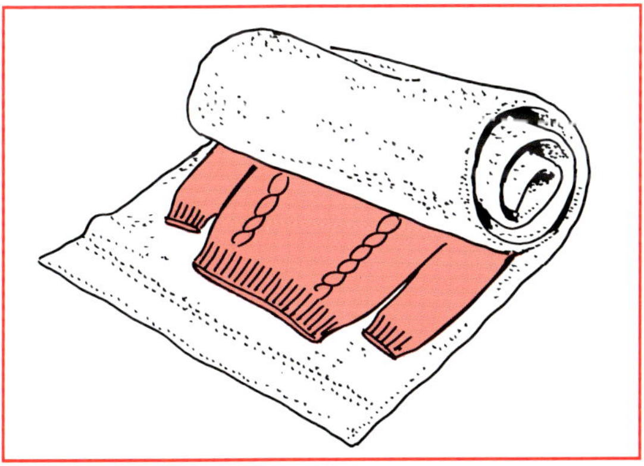

Take as much care drying a piece of crochet as washing. Supporting the weight of the garment, transfer the garment to a colourfast towel and lay it flat. Roll up the towel loosely so that excess moisture is transferred to the towel.

Crocheted work made from natural fibres may be spun dry on a short gentle cycle and it is recommended that cotton is spun as the retained moisture may distort the garment.

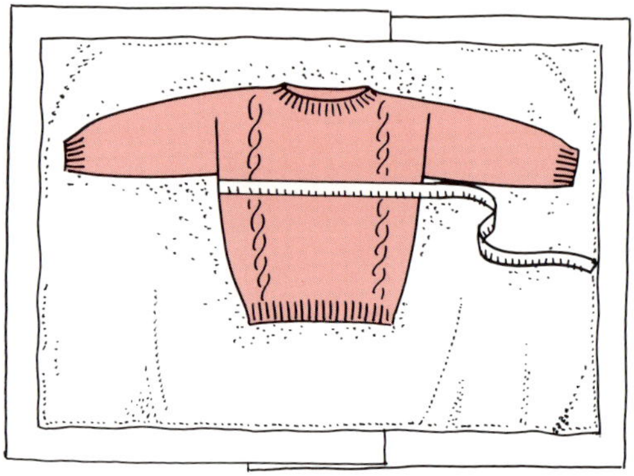

Lightly shake the garment to even out the stitches, lay it on the drying surface and gently reshape it to its original size. Leave the garment until all the excess moisture has been absorbed by the towel. Leave to dry naturally.

Storage

This is equally important. Never hang up a crocheted garment, the weight of the garment pulls it out of shape and the ends of the hanger distort the shapes of the shoulders.

Folding a garment

The following method for folding a sweater gives a neat, space-saving result.

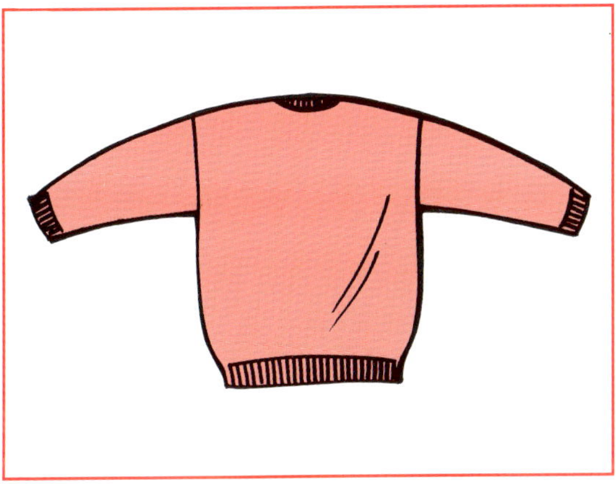

1 Lay the garment on a flat surface with both sleeves fully extended.

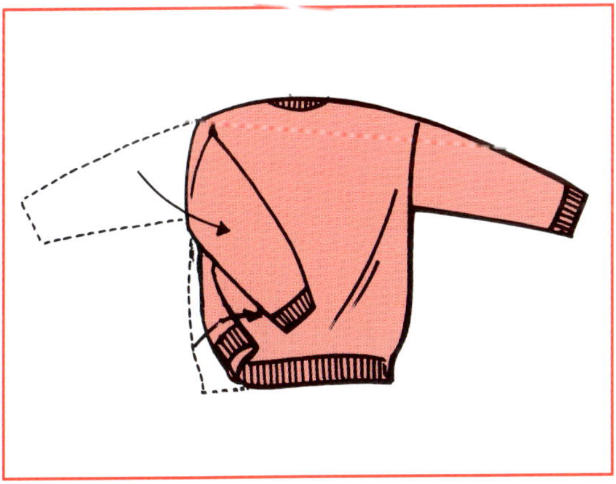

2 Fold in one sleeve diagonally to the side of the garment.

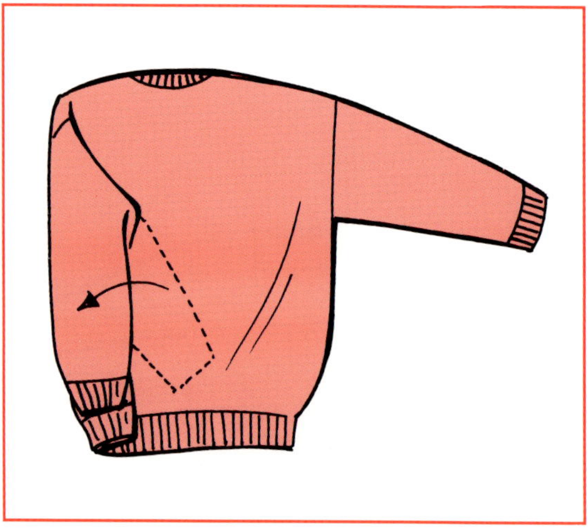

3 Double the sleeve back to form a straight side edge.

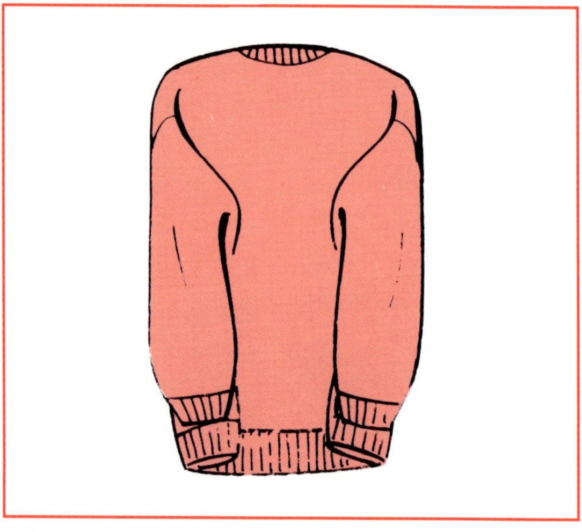

4 Repeat steps 2 and 3 to fold in the other sleeve.

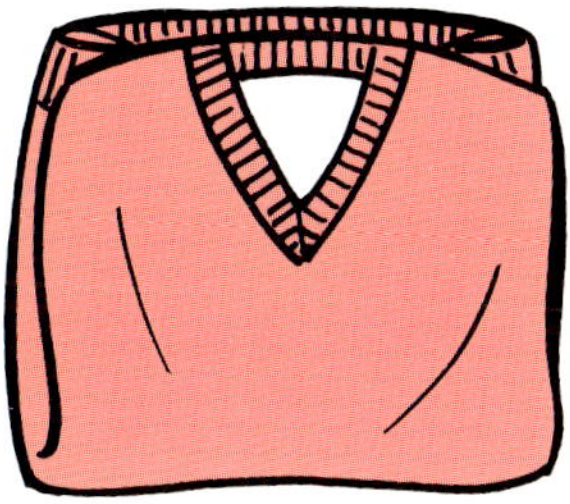

5 Fold the garment in half and store.

If the garment is to be stored for a long time, interleave tissue paper in the garment when folding and place the garment in a plastic bag aerated with plenty of holes.

Index